W9-BVN-421

IT CAN HAPPEN HERE

Also by Joe Conason

*The Raw Deal: How the Bush Republicans Plan to
Destroy Social Security and the Legacy of the New Deal*

*Big Lies: The Right-Wing Propaganda Machine
and How It Distorts the Truth*

*The Hunting of the President: The Ten-Year Campaign
to Destroy Bill and Hillary Clinton*
(with Gene Lyons)

JOE CONASON

IT CAN
HAPPEN
HERE

Authoritarian Peril
in the Age of Bush

THOMAS DUNNE BOOKS ✿ ST. MARTIN'S PRESS
New York

THOMAS DUNNE BOOKS.
An imprint of St. Martin's Press.

www.thomasdunnebooks.com
www.stmartins.com

Library of Congress Cataloging-in-Publication Data

Conason, Joe.
    It can happen here : authoritarian peril in the age of Bush / Joe Conason.—1st ed.
        p. cm.
    Includes bibliographical references and index.
    ISBN-13: 978-0-312-35605-7
    ISBN-10: 0-312-35605-6
    1. United States—Politics and government—2001–2. Authoritarianism—United States. 3. Democracy—United States. 4. Bush, George W. (George Walker), 1946—Political and social views. 5. Conservatism—United States. 6. Big business—Political aspects—United States. 7. Right-wing extremists—United States. I. Title.
    E902.C658 2007
    973.93—dc22

                                        2006035643

First Edition: February 2007

10 9 8 7 6 5 4 3 2 1

For Elizabeth

CONTENTS

ACKNOWLEDGMENTS

To write a book accusing the president and his party of authoritarian ambitions is to invite equally pointed criticism and perhaps angry denunciation. In acknowledging those who helped in this endeavor, I want to express my gratitude without implicating anyone else in my errors or even my opinions. All the credit must be shared, but the blame is all mine.

Thomas Dunne, the publisher of this book as well as *The Hunting of the President* and *Big Lies*, once more conceived a clever title that challenged me to produce a compelling argument. I want to thank Mark LaFlaur, the editor who handled this manuscript with great care and professionalism, and Sean Desmond, my former editor, who left St. Martin's Press while this project was under way. I also appreciate the contributions of assistant editor Benjamin Hart, production editor Kenneth J. Silver, production manager Eric Gladstone, text designer Nicola Ferguson, and jacket designer Jennifer Elaine Huntsman, as well as Mark A. Fowler of Satterlee Stephens Burke & Burke, whose thoughtful legal advice improved the text.

I am still fortunate enough to be represented by Andrew Wylie and Jeffrey Posternak of the Wylie Agency, my advocates and friends.

I must again express gratitude to my colleagues at *Salon.com* for their patience, encouragement, and general excellence, including editor-in-chief Joan Walsh, Michal Keeley, Kerry Lauerman, and Mark Schone. For similar reasons I also owe thanks to my colleagues at the *New York Observer*, including editor Peter W. Kaplan, Tom McGeveran, Terry Golway, Josh Benson, Brian Kempner, and Barry Lewis. I remain especially grateful to former publisher Arthur L. Carter, who entrusted the stewardship of the newspaper he created to Jared Kushner as I was completing this book.

And I should extend appreciation to former colleagues at *The American Prospect*, where I had the pleasure for the past two years of working with my talented friend Michael Tomasky, who stepped down as the magazine's editor last autumn.

As usual, many people graciously assisted with advice, research, clippings, and miscellaneous requests: Don Babets, Bill Babiskin, Tamara Baker, Peter Bloch, Dan Buck, Alan Gilbert, Linda Healey, Jesse Kornbluth and Karen Collins, Mark Karlin, Maria Leavey, Rob Levine, Mark Crispin Miller, Alfred Ross, Martin Rosenblatt, Julia Sneeringer, and Jay Winer. I owe special thanks to my former editorial assistant Evie Nagy. And I must also single out Scott Horton, the "obscure New York attorney" whose courageous defense of human and constitutional rights and spirited, erudite commentary on current events have been an enormous inspiration to me in recent years.

This book was informed by the work of many writers: Mike Allen, Jonathan Alter, Eric Alterman, William Arkin, Russ Baker, Jack Balkin, James Bamford, Alan Berlow, Duncan

Acknowledgments

Black, Max Blumenthal, Sidney Blumenthal, Kristen Breitweiser, David Brock, Ron Brownstein, Frederick Clarkson, Steve Clemons, David Cole, Nicholas Confessore, David Corn, John W. Dean, E. J. Dionne, Robert Dreyfuss, Kevin Drum, Shadia B. Drury, Nina Easton, Thomas Edsall, James Fallows, Bruce Fein, Jamison Foser, Al Franken, Barton Gellman, Robert George, Alan Gilbert, Paul Glastris, Michelle Goldberg, Mark Green, David Greenberg, Jacob Hacker, Nat Hentoff, Hendrik Hertzberg, Stephen Holmes, J. Hoberman, Scott Horton, Mark Hosenball, Arianna Huffington, Michael Isikoff, Molly Ivins, John B. Judis, Fred Kaplan, Harvey J. Kaye, David D. Kirkpatrick, Paul Krugman, Howard Kurtz, Judd Legum, Gene Lyons, Joshua Micah Marshall, Jane Mayer, Harold Meyerson, Mark Crispin Miller, Bill Minutaglio, James Moore, Anne C. Mulkern, David Neiwert, the late Jack Newfield, John Nichols, Timothy Noah, Robert Parry, Rick Perlstein, Paul Pierson, Kevin Phillips, Walter Pincus, Sarah Posner, Dana Priest, Sam Rosenfeld, Laura Rozen, Charlie Savage, Robert Scheer, Kim Lane Scheppele, David Sirota, Wayne Slater, Paul Starr, Peter H. Stone, Andrew Sullivan, Cass R. Sunstein, Ron Suskind, Jeffrey Toobin, Craig Unger, Sean Wilentz, George Will, James Wolcott, Matthew Yglesias, and Markos Moulitsas Zuniga.

My research also benefited greatly from publicly available reports produced by the staff of Representative Henry Waxman, the remarkable California Democrat who may be the single most indefatigable public servant in the United States Congress; and from the indispensable library maintained by Thomas Blanton, Malcolm Byrne, Peter Kornbluh, and the staff and fellows of the National Security Archive at George Washington University.

I could not have completed this book without the warm support of family and friends. Gail Furman generously provided a

xi

beautiful place to think and write while I completed this book. She is a dedicated partisan of democracy whose friendship and counsel have become invaluable to me. For reasons that each of them knows very well, I am also deeply grateful to Wally and Celia Gilbert, Teddy Gross and Ruth Nass, Steve Jones, Andy Karsch and Nan Richardson, John and Symmie Newhouse, Julie Conason and Geoff Bryant, and John R. Wagley Sr. and Jean de la Poer.

Finally there is and will always be Elizabeth Wagley—my wife, my friend, my treasured critic, and my daily inspiration. While this project was under way we literally worked next to each other and have endured many things together during the past year. She surely understands why this book must be dedicated to her. So I'm glad that she likes it.

—November 2006

When fascism comes to America, it will be wrapped in the flag, carrying a cross.

—SINCLAIR LEWIS, author of *It Can't Happen Here* (1935)

IT CAN HAPPEN HERE

INTRODUCTION

IT'S (STILL) A FREE COUNTRY

Those who would give up Essential Liberty to purchase a little
Temporary Safety deserve neither Liberty nor Safety.
—BENJAMIN FRANKLIN

CAN IT HAPPEN here? Is it happening here already? That depends, as a recent president might have said, on what the meaning of "it" is.

To Sinclair Lewis, who sardonically titled his 1935 dystopian novel *It Can't Happen Here*, "it" plainly meant an American version of the totalitarian dictatorships that had seized power in Germany and Italy. Married at the time to the pioneering reporter Dorothy Thompson, who had been expelled from Berlin by the Nazis a year earlier and quickly became one of America's most outspoken critics of fascism, Lewis was acutely aware of the domestic and foreign threats to American freedom. So often did he and Thompson discuss the crisis in Europe and the implications of Europe's fate for the Depression-wracked United States that, according to his biographer, Mark Schorer, Lewis referred to the entire topic somewhat contemptuously as "it."

Fearful of what might come in the next election, he cranked out the pages of *It Can't Happen Here* in a three-month summer sprint between May and August. Whatever his political potboiler lacked in literary merit—Lewis himself rather harshly dismissed it as a "bad book" in private—was more than compensated by its stunning public impact. His burbling, oddly lyrical narration cannot match George Orwell's bleak elegance in *Nineteen Eighty-Four* or Philip Roth's ominous realism in *The Plot Against America*. Yet Americans were fascinated by Lewis's vision of a clownish, sinister, and brutal homegrown fascism, spurred by patriots and preachers. They made his "bad" book into an extraordinary success for publisher Doubleday, which sold more than 300,000 copies in the United States and many thousands more in Britain and France (*Impossible Ici!*), although not in Germany, where the Nazi regime banned it. The U.S. sales alone were roughly the equivalent of selling a million hardcover copies today.

The Metro-Goldwyn-Mayer movie studio quickly optioned the book and commissioned a script in January 1936—and just as quickly abandoned the project two months later, under murky circumstances. According to some accounts, the censors at Hollywood's infamous Hays Office refused to approve the film because of potential international complications and a reluctance to irritate the Republican Party, some of whose leaders were suspected of fascist sympathies, in an election year. Others blamed the studio, whose management apparently feared a total boycott by Germany and Italy if the Lewis film were made. Both governments publicly applauded the decision to kill the project. The production's cancellation and the controversy over the Nazi intimidation of M-G-M created still another burst of publicity.

The political sensation didn't end there. While *It Can't Happen Here* remained at the top of the bestseller lists during the summer and fall of 1936, Lewis collaborated with the Works Progress Administration's Federal Theater to transform the novel into a play, which was eventually produced on Broadway and in more than a score of other venues in a dozen cities. Lewis himself appeared in at least one production, starring as Doremus Jessup, the Vermont newspaper editor who serves as the novel's protagonist. Although critics found his amateur performance engaging, they didn't care much for the play—but that didn't matter any more than the mediocre quality of the book. In various productions, *It Can't Happen Here* notched 260 weeks on stage, or the equivalent of a five-year theatrical run.

For the liberal audience of the thirties, whose patience with charlatans of the extreme right and the Communist left was wearing thin, Lewis cut with a mocking, incredulous edge. A nonideological skeptic, bemused and mildly cynical yet still patriotic and idealistic, he approached politics in much the same spirit as *The Daily Show* or *The Colbert Report* decades later. Indeed, it's easy to imagine Jon Stewart leafing through the pages of *It Can't Happen Here* with terror on his face, as he begins to realize that in certain strange ways, what the long-dead Lewis foresaw seems to resonate now.

DOES ANY OF this sound familiar?

Buzz Windrip, a charismatic politician with little intellectual curiosity but great capacity to appeal to the regular guy, is elected president. Lewis describes him as a "Professional Common Man," with "every prejudice and aspiration of every American Common Man." Among other things, Windrip believes firmly in "the superiority of anyone who possessed a million dollars" and considers all foreigners, "possibly excepting the British," to be degenerate. He is resolutely anti-intellectual, flattering the ignorance of his followers and presenting himself as an exponent of traditional values, liberty, democracy, righteousness, and godliness.

Windrip regularly expresses contempt for the press (except for the newspapers of the ultraright Hearst empire), excoriating newspaper editors as "men without thought of Family or Public Interest or the humble delights of jaunts out-of-doors, plotting how they can put over their lies, and advance their own positions and fill their greedy pocketbooks by calumniating Statesmen." He redefines liberal, in those days a term of praise rather than abuse, into its opposite (much as conservative has lately been changed into something very different under the rubric of "neoconservatism").

· · ·

WINDRIP IS ENTIRELY the creation of Lee Sarason, a brilliant, ruthless strategist and advertising man who has been preparing this presidential campaign behind the scenes for several years. His candidate exudes a syrupy compassion for the white, Christian, middle-class family while proclaiming a staunch moral and patriotic conservatism. He often mentions that he has read the Bible at least a dozen times. His most important supporters are the nation's religious fundamentalists, notably a radio preacher with millions of followers who hails Windrip as God's chosen leader, and the country's wealthiest businessmen, who understand that he is their wholly owned instrument despite his populist rhetoric.

"Oh, I can't tell if he's a crook or a religious fanatic," exclaims Jessup, while listening to the convention proceedings that will nominate Windrip on the Democratic ticket. Yet even Jessup is bamboozled by the candidate's personality when he first sees Windrip speaking in Madison Square Garden. "I'll be hanged!" the momentarily dazzled editor tells himself. "Why, he's a darn good sort when you come to meet him! And warmhearted."

This sense of comfort is an illusion, of course, created by Sarason and Windrip, as is their religiosity. Soon after taking office, they seize upon the genuine economic crisis besetting the country to arrogate more and more power to the White House. Windrip turns Congress into an advisory body and starts appointing pliable hacks to the courts. Acting upon the assumption that constitutional procedures are a dangerous barrier to executive action, he swiftly dismantles them.

His government conducts business in near-total secrecy, acting to suppress or control the press while the right-wing Hearst media serve as propaganda outlets for the Windrip administration, lavishing praise upon the president and all his works, including his plans for a preemptive war on Mexico. As he explains, there is no need for a free and informed press, run by "those smart alecks in New York and Washington," because "it is not fair to ordinary folks—it just confuses them—to try to make them swallow all the true facts that would be suitable to a higher class of people."

His economic policies derive from impossible campaign promises to provide generous benefits without raising taxes to pay for them, even as the military is built up for aggressive war. He gradually bankrupts the country while the wealthy few at the top grow wealthier. Despite his pledges of equality, the tax system becomes increasingly regressive while wages are driven inexorably downward. Any citizen who dares to question the new order, such as Doremus Jessup, is eventually brought before a military tribunal to answer charges of treason.

In *Zero Hour*, the campaign book ghostwritten for him by Sarason—Windrip's brain—he offers fair warning of the improvements he plans to bring to constitutional government. "I want to stand up on my hind legs, and not just admit but frankly holler right out that . . . we've got to change our system a lot, maybe even change the whole Constitution. . . . The Executive has got to have a freer hand and be able to move quick in an emergency, and not be tied down by dumb shyster lawyer congressmen taking months to shoot off their mouths in debates."

Windrip's seizure of power culminates in the utter suppression of dissent, the complete abrogation of the Bill of Rights, the establishment of labor and detention camps where prisoners are regularly murdered or kept under the filthiest conditions, and the violent suppression of labor unions and political rivals by Windrip's Corporatists, or Corpos, as they come to be known. Doremus Jessup is arrested for sedition and eventually incarcerated in a camp, from which he flees to join the underground resistance led by the book's true hero, Walt Trowbridge—the honest, Lincolnesque senator who had run against Windrip in the 1936 election, and who has escaped to Canada to mount a rebellion against the Corpos. Trowbridge is an old-style Republican who loves the Constitution and hates authoritarianism.

IF "IT" DENOTES the police state American-style as imagined and satirized by Lewis, complete with concentration camps, martial law, and mass executions of strikers and other dissidents, then "it" hasn't happened here and isn't likely to happen anytime soon.

For contemporary Americans, however, "it" could signify our own more gradual and insidious turn toward authoritarian rule. That is why Lewis's darkly funny but grim fable of an authoritarian coup achieved through a democratic election still resonates today—along with all the eerie parallels between what he imagined then and what we live with now.

While the specific elements of It Can't Happen Here were obviously designed to parody events and personalities of the 1930s, the author of Babbitt and Elmer Gantry was also delivering a deeper warning about American values and the vulnerability of democratic institutions to right-wing demagoguery, corporate manipulation, and public apathy. Lewis, the first American winner of the Nobel Prize for Literature, did not aspire to write agitprop, although he wasn't ashamed to use his fame and skills in the service of his politics (which at the time meant supporting Franklin D. Roosevelt and the New Deal).

Certainly he was trying to say more than simply to beware the bullying ambitions of Louisiana governor and senator Huey Long, who was assassinated before the book was published. He believed that the roots of authoritarianism had been firmly planted in our political culture by the beginning of the last century—and that throughout human history all peoples and civilizations eventually have been tempted by tyrants, and most have succumbed to their blandishments. As he pointed out, there was no shortage of evidence in our own history that Americans were subject to the same passions and prejudices that had led other peoples to surrender their freedom. They had been lucky enough and brave enough to escape that fate. And in the time of crisis, when powerful figures in the corporate elite and the Republican Party looked toward fascism for salvation, the American people chose democracy and the New Deal instead.

FOR THE FIRST time since the resignation of Richard M. Nixon more than three decades ago, Americans have had reason to doubt the future of democracy and the rule of law in our own country. Today we live in a state of tension between the enjoyment of traditional freedoms, including the protections afforded to speech and person by the Bill of Rights, and the disturbing realization that those freedoms have been undermined and may be abrogated at any moment.

Such foreboding, which would have been dismissed as paranoia not so long ago, has been intensified by the unfolding crisis of political legitimacy in the capital. George W. Bush has repeatedly asserted and exercised authority that he does not possess under the Constitution he swore to uphold. He has announced that he intends to continue exercising power according to his claim of a mandate that erases the separation and balancing of power among the branches of government, frees him from any real obligation to obey laws passed by Congress, and permits him to ignore any provisions of the Bill of Rights that may prove inconvenient.

Whether his fellow Americans understand exactly what Bush is doing or not, his six years in office have created intense public anxiety. Much of that anxiety can be attributed to fear of terrorism, which Bush has exacerbated to suit his own purposes—as well as to increasing concern that the world is threatened by global warming, pandemic diseases, economic insecurity, nuclear proliferation, and other perils with which this presidency cannot begin to cope.

As the midterm election showed, more and more Americans realize that something has gone far wrong at the highest levels of government and politics—that Washington's one-party regime had created a daily spectacle of stunning incompetence and dishonesty. Pollsters have found large majorities of voters worrying that the country is on the wrong track. At this writing, two of every three voters give that answer, and they are not just anxious but furious. Almost half are willing to endorse the censure of the president.

Suspicion and alienation extend beyond the usual disgruntled Democrats to independents and even a significant minority of Republicans. A surprisingly large segment of the electorate is willing to contemplate the possibility of impeaching the president, unappetizing though that prospect should be to anyone who can recall the destructive impeachment of Bush's predecessor.

The reasons for popular disenchantment with the Republican regime are well known—from the misbegotten, horrifically mismanaged war in Iraq to the heartless mishandling of the Hurricane Katrina disaster. In both instances, growing anger over the damage done to the national interest and the loss of life and treasure has been exacerbated by evidence of bad faith—by lies, cronyism, and corruption.

Everyone knows—although not everyone necessarily wishes to acknowledge—that the Bush administration misled the American people about the true purposes and likely costs of invading Iraq. It invented a mortal threat to the nation in order to justify illegal aggression. It has repeatedly sought, from the beginning, to exploit the state of war for partisan advantage and presidential image management. It has wasted billions of dollars, and probably tens of billions, on Pentagon contractors with patronage connections to the Republican Party.

Everyone knows, too, that the administration dissembled about the events leading up to the destruction of New Orleans. Its negligence and obliviousness in the wake of the storm were shocking, as was its attempt to conceal its errors. It has yet to explain why a person with few discernible qualifications, other than his status as a crony and business associate of his predecessor, was directing the Federal Emergency Management Agency. By elevating ethically dubious, inexperienced, and ineffectual management the administration compromised a critical agency that had functioned brilliantly during the Clinton administration.

To date, however, we do not know the full dimensions of the scandals behind Iraq and Katrina, because the Republican leaders of the Senate and the House of Representatives abdicated the traditional congressional duties of oversight and investigation. It is due to their dereliction that neither the president nor any of his associates have seemed even mildly chastened in the wake of catastrophe. With a single party monopolizing power yet evading responsibility, there was nobody with the constitutional power to hold the White House accountable.

Bolstered by political impunity, especially in a time of war, perhaps any group of politicians would be tempted to abuse power. But this party and these politicians, unchecked by normal democratic constraints, proved to be particularly dangerous. The name for what is wrong with them—the threat embedded within the Bush administration, the Republican congressional leadership, and the current leaders of the Republican Party—is *authoritarianism.*

The most obvious symptoms can be observed in the regime's style, which features an almost casual contempt for democratic and lawful norms; an expanding appetite for executive control at the expense of constitutional balances; a reckless impulse to corrupt national institutions with partisan ideology; and an ugly tendency to smear dissent as disloyalty. The most troubling effects are matters of substance, including the suspension of traditional legal rights for certain citizens; the imposition of secrecy and the inhibition of the free flow of information; the extension of domestic spying without legal sanction or warrant; the promotion of torture and other barbaric practices, in defiance of American and international law; and the collusion of government and party with corporate interests and religious fundamentalists.

WHAT WORRIES MANY Americans even more is that the authoritarians can excuse their excesses as the necessary response to an enemy that every American knows to be real. For the past five years, the Republican leadership has argued that the attacks of September 11, 2001—and the continuing threat from jihadist groups such as al Qaeda—demand permanent changes in American government, society, and foreign policy. Are those changes essential to preserve our survival—or merely useful for unscrupulous politicians who still hope to achieve permanent domination by their own narrowly ideological party? Not only liberals and leftists, but centrists, libertarians, and conservatives, of every party and no party, have come to distrust the answers given by those in power.

The most salient dissent to be heard in recent years, and especially since Bush's reelection in 2004, has been voiced not by the liberals and moderates who never trusted the Republican leadership, but by conservatives who once did.

Former Republican congressman Bob Barr of Georgia, who served as one of the managers of the impeachment of Bill Clinton in the House of Representatives, has joined the American Civil Liberties Union he once detested. In the measures taken by the

Bush administration and approved by his former colleagues, Barr sees the potential for "a totalitarian type regime." Paul Craig Roberts, a longtime contributor to the *Wall Street Journal* and a former Treasury official under Reagan, perceives the "main components of a police state" in the Bush administration's declaration of plenary powers to deny fundamental rights to suspected terrorists. Bruce Fein, who served as associate attorney general in the Reagan Justice Department, believes that the Bush White House is "a clear and present danger to the rule of law," and that the president "cannot be trusted to conduct the war against global terrorism with a decent respect for civil liberties and checks against executive abuses." Syndicated columnist George Will accuses the administration of pursuing a "monarchical doctrine" in its assertion of extraordinary war powers.

In the 2006 midterm election, disenchanted conservatives joined with liberals and centrists to deliver a stinging rebuke to the regime by overturning Republican domination in both houses of Congress. For the first time since 1994, Democrats control the Senate and the House of Representatives. But the Democratic majority in the upper chamber is as narrow as possible, depending on the whims of Joseph Lieberman of Connecticut, a Republican-leaning Democrat elected on an independent ballot line, who has supported the White House on the occupation of Iraq, abuse of prisoners of war, domestic spying, the suspension of habeas corpus, military tribunals, far-right jucicial nominations, and other critical constitutional issues. Nor is Lieberman alone among the Senate Democrats in his supine acquiescence to the abuses of the White House.

Even if the Democrats had won a stronger majority in the Senate, it would be naïve to expect that a single election victory could mend the damage inflicted on America's constitutional fabric during the past six years. While the Bush administration has enjoyed an extraordinary immunity from Congressional oversight until now, the deepest implication of its actions and statements, as explored in the pages that follow, is that neither legislators nor courts can thwart the will of the unitary executive. When Congress challenges that presidential claim, as inevitably it will, than what seems almost certain to follow is not "bipartisanship" but confrontation. The election of 2006 was not an end but another beginning.

The question that we face in the era of terror alerts, religious fundamentalism, and endless warfare is whether we are still the brave nation preserved and rebuilt by the generation of Sinclair Lewis—or whether our courage, and our luck, have finally run out. America is not yet on the verge of fascism, but democracy is again in danger. The striking resemblance between Buzz Windrip and George W. Bush and the similarity of the political forces behind them is more than a literary curiosity. It is a warning on yellowed pages from those to whom we owe everything.

ONE

THE "POST-9/11 WORLDVIEW" OF KARL ROVE

No nation could preserve its freedom in the midst of continual warfare.

—JAMES MADISON

MADISON'S WARNING, DELIVERED during the early years of the American Republic in a congressional debate over presidential powers, has been vindicated many times since then. For reasons that the fourth president could not possibly have foreseen, his observation may be even more urgent now. And when he further observed that war empowers the nation's chief executive with "all the means of seducing the minds . . . of the people," he seemed to anticipate how a modern president might be tempted to exploit a state of "continual warfare"— such as an indefinitely extended "war on terror," also known as "the long war"—to secure political domination.

In American history, authoritarian excess has often accompanied war (or the fear of war), from the Alien and Sedition Acts passed by Madison's political opponents to Abraham Lincoln's Civil War suspension of habeas corpus; from the Red Scare of World War I to the internment of Japanese in World War II; from Joseph McCarthy's depredations at the beginning of the cold war to Richard Nixon's abuses during the war in Vietnam.

Those wartime encroachments eventually receded, owing to the end of hostilities or the vitality of democratic resistance. But what would happen in a nation beset by continual warfare? How will liberty and democracy survive what the Pentagon and the president predict will be decades of a long war against terror?

In literature, too, war has been depicted as the precondition for dictatorship. Two of the twentieth century's most celebrated authors imagined totalitarian societies in which permanent warfare could become the most effective instrument of control. In their very different novels about societies without freedom, Sinclair Lewis and George Orwell portrayed politicians who misled their countries into aggressive military conflict for ulterior motives. The central fact of life in Orwell's *Nineteen Eighty-Four* is a perpetual and perplexing battle among three superstates, which may or may not be waged largely for the sake of brainwashing and subduing their own peoples. The action takes place in London, and Orwell's masterpiece is not only a denunciation of Soviet and Nazi totalitarianism, but a warning about what all modern societies were in danger of becoming.

More than a decade earlier, Lewis satirically depicted the exploitation of the same bloody means to achieve a nefarious end in *It Can't Happen Here*—a story set in the United States. He imagined an elected dictatorship fabricating bogus provocations that would allow America to wage a preemptive war against Mexico. The author of this plan is a presidential adviser who bears a startling resemblance to a certain contemporary figure in attitude, influence, and proximity to the president. It is this crafty, ruthless adviser, Lee Sarason, the creator of President Berzelius "Buzz" Windrip, who first articulates how and why war will prove indispensable to the new regime.

Holding forth in a cabinet meeting, Sarason "demanded that, in order to bring and hold all elements in the country together by that useful Patriotism which always appears upon threat of an outside attack, the government immediately arrange to be insulted and menaced in a well-planned series of deplorable 'incidents' on the Mexican border, and declare war on Mexico as soon as America showed that it was getting hot and patriotic enough."

Sarason's scheme elicits an enthusiastic response from Hector Macgoblin, the secretary of education and public relations, a burly boxing fan and nationalistic bully with multiple doctoral degrees (a character who could have been based on radio blowhard William Bennett, the former drug czar and education secretary). He points out that in the past "governments had merely let themselves slide into war," but that "in this age of deliberate, planned propaganda, a really modern government . . . must figure out what brand of war they had to sell and plan the selling campaign consciously."

That scenario will seem startlingly contemporary to anyone who remembers the campaign to sell the invasion of Iraq—including the role of Karl Rove and the White House Iraq Group. That infamous selling campaign was announced in September 2002 by White House chief of staff Andrew Card, who breezily explained the administration's timing to the press. "From a marketing point of view," quipped Card, a former auto industry lobbyist, "you don't introduce new products in August."

Now, more than four years later, most of that product's regretful buyers have been left wondering what the sellers were actually selling. By now everyone knows that the purposes proclaimed by the Bush administration at the time of the invasion—to rid Iraq of actual and potential weapons of mass destruction—were fraudulent. Moreover, everyone also knows that during the months leading up to the invasion, the president and his closest advisers were aware that the alleged facts justifying war "had been fixed," as the British intelligence chief noted in the famous "Downing Street memo" of July 2002. Some analysts believed that the objective of the war was to gain control of Iraqi oil, although Saddam Hussein had always been willing to sell petroleum to the West at the world price. Others suggested that Iraq was an easy target for the assertion of U.S. military force at a critical moment. And still others insisted that invading Iraq was merely the first stage of a broader plan to remake the Middle East by force that had long been mulled by neoconservative ideologues.

The decision to go to war probably reflects all those elements, but the question of its timing remains. Why introduce this controversial "new product" in September 2002, only weeks before the midterm elections? Why call for a congressional vote authorizing the use of military force against Iraq that autumn? With that demand, Bush reversed the path his father had taken in preparation for the Gulf War in 1990, asking Congress for authorization only after the U.N. Security Council acted first.

Several months earlier, Karl Rove had hinted at the real reason for the rush to war. For this architect of conservative power, with his ambition to inaugurate a generation or more of Republican political domination, the second year of George W. Bush's first term was a critical and dangerous time. He needed to win the midterm elections, against the historical odds—and nothing would unify the country behind the presidential party like the force of war.

Rove, the powerful "Mayberry Machiavelli" who merged policy with politics in the Bush White House, had closely monitored the effect of war on the domestic political fortunes of his patrons. In 1991, he had observed the first President Bush's popularity rocket upward during the first Gulf War. A decade later he had watched as the approval ratings of his boss, the second President Bush, reached even more impressive heights as he commanded the overthrow of the Taliban. Yet he could also recall how the popularity of the first President Bush plunged after the Gulf War troops came home—and he had measured the ratings of the second President Bush as they dwindled almost thirty points between September 2001 and August 2002.

That is why Bush and Rove departed so radically from the conduct of past wartime presidencies, which struggled to bring the entire nation together against the enemy. Using war to cement Republican political domination means dividing, not uniting.

. . .

KARL ROVE RARELY indulges any urge to speak publicly. He knows his own limitations and tends to remain in cloistered offices and back rooms, quite distant from the dangerous limelight. Yet although he is neither an inspiring nor a charismatic speaker, he understands the power of a simple message that is repeated again and again. On the few occasions over the past several years when he has spoken out, Rove has struck a single chord with growing intensity. His message could be summarized in this way:

America is at war. It is a war that will continue indefinitely. Republicans and conservatives possess the moral strength to fight and win, while Democrats and liberals do not. Therefore, the survival of the nation requires that the Republican Party maintain a monopoly of power.

To Rove this simple equation represents "the post-9/11 worldview." In his world, it is the only valid worldview. He may not fully believe every word of it; in fact, he knows from his own experience that its characterization of Democrats and liberals is false, but that scarcely matters. For him the equation is true in a much deeper sense, because it served Rove's self-appointed mission of establishing Republican hegemony.

The first indication that Rove planned to turn the war on terror into an assault on the loyal opposition came during January 2002, in a speech to the winter conference of the Republican National Committee in Austin, Texas. With President George W. Bush riding a powerful wave of public support and bipartisan unity, his chief political strategist had returned to Texas to discuss the upcoming midterm congressional elections with party leaders.

Only months earlier, on the steps of the Capitol, the nation's elected representatives, from the most liberal Democrats to the most conservative Republicans, had promised to stand with the president against the terrorists who had destroyed the World

Trade Center and attacked the Pentagon. "We want America to speak with one voice tonight and we want enemies and the whole world and all of our citizens to know that America speaks tonight with one voice," said Richard Gephardt, then the House Democratic leader. Tom Daschle, then the Senate Democratic leader, stood with his Republican counterpart, Trent Lott, in a display of unqualified support for the president. "We want President Bush to know—we want the world to know—that he can depend on us," declared Daschle.

Those faithful pledges—fulfilled in unquestioning cooperation with every legislative and budgetary request from the White House, including the rapid passage of the USA Patriot Act—meant nothing to Rove. He was looking ahead to November 2002, when he hoped to score a historic victory that would prove the nation's ideological realignment to the right and mark a milestone for Rove and the generation of right-wing zealots who acknowledge him as their leader. Back then, Grover Norquist, the preeminent conservative strategist, lobbyist, and antitax activist who has known and worked with Rove since they were leaders of the College Republicans, articulated their ultimate objective. "It isn't our job to seek peaceful coexistence with the left. Our job is to remove them from power permanently."

More than taxes, race, abortion, or any of the perennial grievances of the right, permanent war seemed to provide the most compelling means to achieve that lifelong goal.

In Austin, Rove told his fellow Republicans, "We can go to the country on this issue, because they trust the Republican Party to do a better job of protecting and strengthening America's military might and thereby protecting America." Those bland phrases hardly reflected his real feelings and intentions. The ensuing campaign against Democratic incumbents included some of the most vicious advertising deployed in many years, with Daschle portrayed as a stooge of the al Qaeda terrorists and Senator Max Cleland, a triple amputee Vietnam war hero and winner of the Bronze Star and the Silver Star, derided as unpatriotic. Both lost their reelection bids.

Damaging as the midterm campaign was to national morale, at a time when unity should have been paramount, Rove's strategy was nevertheless brilliantly successful. The Republicans carried the same precepts forward into the 2004 presidential campaign, which featured the gross exploitation of the 9/11 attacks in advertising and at the GOP convention in New York; an outrageous smear of the patriotism and navy service of Democratic nominee John Kerry; a series of conveniently timed terror alerts leading up to Election Day; and repeated warnings by Vice President Dick Cheney and other party spokesmen that a Democratic victory would signal weakness to the terrorists who are waiting to strike again.

The following summer, as the reelected president's ratings plunged along with popular support for the war in Iraq, Rove returned to the same theme with still greater ferocity. On June 22, 2005, he addressed the annual dinner of the New York State Conservative Party—a third party founded by members of the Buckley family and run by hard-line ideologues who consider the state's Republican Party much too moderate.

Rove had traveled north to accept the Conservative Party's Charles Edison Award. This special honor is named for a deceased New Jersey governor and industrialist who also happened to have been among the first prominent endorsers of the ultraright extremist John Birch Society, which smeared President Dwight D. Eisenhower as a Communist traitor.

That old Birch mind-set seemed to have inspired Rove's remarks.

He opened with a few bland paragraphs of congratulation, hailing the great strides in recent decades by Republicans and conservatives, and noting their traditional disagreements with liberals over tax cuts and the role of government. But he had come to dinner to serve red meat, not pablum. First he declared that "the most important difference between conservatives and liberals can be found in the area of national security." Then he launched a savagely sarcastic attack on the character of every liberal American and most Democrats:

"Conservatives saw the savagery of the 9/11 attacks and prepared for war, liberals saw the savagery of the 9/11 attacks and wanted to prepare indictments and offer therapy and understanding for our attackers. In the wake of 9/11, conservatives believed it was time to unleash the might and power of the United States military against the Taliban; in the wake of 9/11, liberals believed it was time to . . . submit a petition. I am not joking. Submitting a petition is precisely what [the progressive grassroots organization] Moveon.org did. It was a petition imploring the 'powers that be' to 'use moderation and restraint in responding to the . . . terrorist attacks against the United States.'

"I don't know about you," Rove continued, "but moderation and restraint is not what I felt as I watched the Twin Towers crumble to the earth; a side of the Pentagon destroyed; and almost 3,000 of our fellow citizens perish in flames and rubble.

"Moderation and restraint is not what I felt—and moderation and restraint is not what was called for. It was a moment to summon our national will—and to brandish steel."

The only steel Rove had ever brandished was a fork, but that didn't slow him down.

"MoveOn.org, Michael Moore, and Howard Dean may not have agreed with this, but the American people did. Conservatives saw what happened to us on 9/11 and said: we will defeat our enemies. Liberals saw what happened to us and said: we must understand our enemies. Conservatives see the United States as a great nation engaged in a noble cause; liberals see the United States and they see . . . Nazi concentration camps, Soviet gulags, and the killing fields of Cambodia."

This was the legendary dirty fighter of American politics, deliberately distorting the views of liberals and Democrats, freely fabricating "facts" to slander his opponents. He knew that no liberals had urged therapy or understanding for the hijackers. He knew that Moveon.org, with millions of progressive citizens organized via the Internet, had never circulated any petition demanding restraint against the Taliban. He knew there was no evidence that Howard Dean, the Democratic Party chairman, had opposed the war in Afghanistan or urged "understanding" for al Qaeda. He knew that liberals didn't regard America as the equivalent of Nazi or Communist totalitarians. (That crack referred to a floor speech by Senator Dick Durbin of Illinois, the Democratic whip, lamenting the mistreatment of detainees in the military camps at Guantánamo Bay, as revealed in a declassified FBI report.) As Rove well knew, the truth was that the vast majority of American liberals and progressives, including Dean and Durbin and the members of Moveon.org, had concurred with the president in his decision to invade Afghanistan and overthrow the Taliban.

Rove knew, in fact, that the liberals and Democrats in Congress had stood squarely behind Bush in the decision to extirpate the Taliban and destroy al Qaeda. Their only disappointment was that he had done the job so hesitantly and ineptly, allowing Osama bin Laden and Mullah Omar to escape.

Rove's Conservative Party speech exemplified the classic rhetorical tactics of authoritarianism, employing innuendo and lies to transform political opponents into soft-minded dupes and potential traitors. After spewing his slanders, he was just clever enough to provide himself with a rhetorical safety net. "At the core, we are dealing with two parties that have fundamentally different views on national security," he said. "Republicans have a post-9/11 worldview and many Democrats have a pre-9/11 worldview. That doesn't make them unpatriotic—not at all. But it does make them wrong—deeply and profoundly and consistently wrong."

It was an audacious lie from beginning to end. But if you believed him, then you would also agree that the Democrats should be disqualified from power for as long as the nation was in danger—and if you believed Bush, that would be a long, long time.

Since Rove delivered that speech, the White House has rebranded its "global war on terror" twice. For a brief period that summer, the war was officially renamed the "global struggle against violent extremism," apparently in belated acknowledgment that political and ideological strategies are just as salient as military power. *Slate* military analyst Fred Kaplan observed in despair that "the driving force behind the new slogan [was] a desire for a happier acronym." What had been GWOT, pronounced "gee-wot," became GSAVE, or "gee-save." That didn't help much.

President Bush more recently said that he thinks of it as World War III, but Norman Podhoretz, the neoconservative literary light and amateur strategic thinker, has suggested that it is really World War IV, because we already fought World War III in the cold war.

In January 2006, a new official name appeared in the Pentagon's *Quadrennial Defense Review*, the strategic planning document issued by the defense secretary every four years. The latest version refers to the struggle against Islamist terrorism as "the long war"—a portentous description that is clearly intended to evoke the cold war's decades of global confrontation. "The struggle . . . may well be fought in dozens of other countries simultaneously and for many years to come," warned the report. By implicitly comparing al Qaeda and its ragtag allies with the massive armed forces of Soviet Communism, Donald Rumsfeld and the neoconservative ideologues who worked for him evidently sought to initiate still another vast enlargement of the defense budget and a greatly expanded American presence overseas. The outcome of this permanent state of war is meant to be American hegemony abroad and conservative domination at home.

HOW AND WHEN Karl Rove came to understand that permanent war could be exploited to advance his political aims is not clear. When the Republican consultant entered the White House in January 2001 with George W. Bush, the candidate he had trained and tutored, the new government's national security policies were vague, to put it politely. The presidential campaign of 2000 had not turned on issues of defense and foreign policy, which was just as well for Bush, who could scarcely articulate an opinion on those topics beyond a few earnest platitudes he had picked up from his advisers.

Bush promised to keep America strong. He would never commit American troops to any conflict abroad without a plan for victory and an exit strategy. At the same time, he voiced support for most recent American military interventions abroad, which he deemed to have served the national interest. (He would always pursue the national interest, of course.) He would approach other countries with humility and shun foolhardy, excessively ambitious nation-building projects.

"I'm worried about overcommitting our military around the world. I want to be judicious in its use," said Bush during his second debate with Vice President Al Gore on October 12, 2000. "I'm not so sure the role of the United States is to go around the world and say this is the way it's got to be." His cautious endorsements of traditional Republican pragmatism and multilateralism offered no notion of what was to come.

Exactly three months and eight days after that innocuous debate, in which Bush could scarcely be distinguished from Gore, the newly inaugurated president and the members of his National Security Council sat down for their first official meeting. Among those present was Treasury Secretary Paul O'Neill, whose firing less than two years later would eventually provoke him to reveal what he had witnessed in the Bush White House. According to O'Neill, the first topic on the agenda of that initial meeting was the invasion and occupation of Iraq.

Briefing materials for that meeting included a "Plan for Post-Saddam Iraq," which included a period of peacekeeping by U.S. soldiers, a war crimes tribunal for Saddam and other Baath Party officials, and a scheme (with maps) for exploiting Iraq's oil resources. Support for regime change in Iraq dated back to 1998, when Saddam forced the U.N. weapons inspection team to leave the country. But President Bill Clinton had not sought an excuse to mount an invasion. Bush told his aides that he wanted an excuse to attack.

"It was all about finding a way to do it. That was the tone of it. The president saying 'Go find me a way to do this,'" O'Neill recalled. The tone of the discussion, which continued two days later, was that the United States would sooner or later act unilaterally against the regime of Saddam Hussein. The emerging contours of Bush foreign policy bore no resemblance to the humble, practical approach promised during the campaign.

The motivations behind the real policy were mixed.

Many of the key advisers to Cheney and Rumsfeld were neoconservatives who had advocated forcible regime change in Iraq long before Bush became president. They had been associated with the Project for the New American Century, the think tank set up by neoconservative editor William Kristol to promote an aggressive, militaristic American foreign policy, with emphasis on action in the Middle East against regimes hostile to the United States and Israel. In keeping with that outlook, former Halliburton president Cheney and his allies in the energy industry seemed to look forward to new opportunities in the Iraqi oil fields.

For the president and his chief adviser Rove, the political motives to go to war may well have been the most compelling. *Houston Chronicle* columnist Mickey Herskowitz, a Bush family confidant, revealed in 2004 that George W. Bush and his aides were enthralled with the "political capital" and public glory accruing to leaders like Ronald Reagan, Margaret Thatcher, and the first President Bush, who overpowered smaller adversaries by military force.

Perhaps Rove was familiar with Irving Kristol's 1989 essay on the Grenada invasion, used by Reagan to draw attention away from the disastrous terrorist bombing of a marine barracks in Lebanon. "The reason we gave for the intervention—the risk to American medical students there—was phony but the reaction of the American people was absolutely and overwhelmingly favorable," Kristol gloated in retrospect. "They had no idea what was going on, but they backed the president. They always will." (That MISSION ACCOMPLISHED moment on May 1, 2003, was in the making long before George W. Bush became president.)

"Start a small war," summed up the Bush attitude, as described by Herskowitz. "Pick a country where there is justification you can jump on, go ahead and invade." Herskowitz had conducted nearly twenty interviews with the younger Bush while working on his campaign autobiography in 1999, and the journalist remembered specifically what the Texas governor had said on the subject of war with Iraq.

"One of the keys to being seen as a great leader is to be seen as a commander-in-chief," said Bush, according to Herskowitz. "My father had all this political capital built up when he drove the Iraqis out of Kuwait and he wasted it. . . . If I have a chance to invade, if I had that much capital, I'm not going to waste it. I'm going to get everything passed that I want to get passed and I'm going to have a successful presidency."

The moderate tenor of Bush's campaign speeches on defense and foreign policy during his first presidential campaign had been a ruse, much like his claim to be a new kind of compassionate conservative. Long before September 11, Bush had seen war as an arena to advance his political agenda. The attack by al Qaeda and the alleged threat from Saddam Hussein provided the opportunity he wanted.

As the true time line of the Iraq war is gradually revealed, the political logic of invading as soon as possible becomes clearer. During the summer of 2002, Bush's "successful" presidency was suddenly endangered by the corporate scandals that had first ruined Enron and his friend Kenneth "Kenny Boy" Lay and then engulfed Arthur Andersen, WorldCom, Adelphia, Global Crossing, Tyco, Qwest, Dynegy, and other major firms. By July, the scandal wave was rolling toward the White House, with fresh questions boiling up in the usually placid media about Bush's alleged insider trading at Harken Energy Corporation in 1990, about government sweetheart contracts awarded to Cheney's former employers at Halliburton, and about all those former Enron officials and advisers associated with the White House, including Rove. The stock market index lost nearly a thousand points.

In a column urging the president to invade Iraq immediately—a notion that betrayed profound ignorance of the logistical requirements of modern war—New York Post pundit John Podhoretz bluntly touted the political profit. The excitable son of neoconservative eminence Norman often babbles forth the unspoken (and unspeakable) inner thoughts of his clique.

"There's a luscious double trap in starting the war as soon as possible, Mr. President," he wrote, as if starting a war felt like eating an ice-cream sundae. "Your enemies are delirious with excitement about the corporate-greed scandals and the effect they might have on your popularity and the GOP's standing in November.

"If you get troops on the ground quickly, they will go berserk. Incautious Democrats and liberal pundits will shriek that you've gone to war solely to protect yourself from the corporate-greed scandal. They will forget the lesson they so quickly learned after Sept. 11, which is that at a time of war the American people want their political leaders to stand together.

"Your enemies will hurl ugly accusations at you, Mr. President. And at least one of them will be true—the accusation that you began the war when you did for political reasons.

"But that won't matter. It won't matter to the American people, and it won't matter as far as history is concerned. History will record that you and the U.S. military brought an end to a barbaric regime on its way to threatening the world."

Now, Podhoretz obviously had no clue what his proposal would demand in military terms. Mounting a successful land invasion of a country the size of Iraq takes months, not weeks, especially if the commanders give a damn about the care, feeding, and security of their troops. Stupid as his column was, however, it nevertheless revealed the right-wing appetite for the "luscious" prospect of war. If the president couldn't actually start bombing, he could start beating the war drums. That would distract the public from corporate scandals, too.

Writing in the *New York Times* on July 20, Frank Rich detected the same imperative: "Wagging the dog no longer cuts it. If the Bush administration wants to distract Americans from watching their 401(k)'s go down the toilet, it will have to unleash the whole kennel," he predicted.

So it may not have been pure coincidence that around that same time, Bush accelerated his drive to invade Iraq, according to the "Downing Street memo" setting down the minutes of a British cabinet meeting on July 23, 2002. That memo included the summary of a report by Sir Richard Dearlove, the British intelligence chief, on his recent meetings with Bush administration officials in Washington:

"There was a perceptible shift in attitude. Military action was now seen as inevitable. Bush wanted to remove Saddam, through military action, justified by the conjunction of terrorism and WMD. But the intelligence and facts were being fixed around the policy." The Brits failed to give sufficient weight to the fact that 2002 was an election year in the United States. The policy was being fixed around the politics.

IF THE SEPTEMBER 11 attacks offered the rallying cry for permanent war, then the neoconservatives provided an intellectual underpinning. Led by such veterans of previous Republican administrations as William Kristol, Paul Wolfowitz, Richard Perle, and Elliot Abrams, their Washington infrastructure comprised a very well funded array of major think tanks, including the American Enterprise Institute, the Center for Security Policy, the Project for a New American Century, and the Hudson Institute; magazines including the *Weekly Standard*, the *American Spectator*, and the *National Review*; and an extensive network of writers, scholars, lawyers, government officials, and former officials specializing in national security and foreign affairs. A long list of publicly identified neocons followed Bush and Rove into the power suites of the White House and the Pentagon, where they held strategic positions of authority under Cheney and Rumsfeld.

The neoconservatives advocated an aggressively unipolar defense posture, one that would make the United States an uncontested hegemon with the military capacity to enforce a worldwide Pax Americana. Their strategic thinking—summarized in studies prepared by the Project for the New American Century—imagined a world in which American power could reshape entire regions, especially the Middle East, into arrangements more congenial to the United States and Israel. Urging substantially increased spending on defense production and research, and the militarization of space, they didn't shrink from the likelihood that seeking such unrivaled power would provoke ongoing conflict. Indeed, the more outspoken figures among the neoconservatives welcomed that prospect.

Superficially, at least, the neoconservative ideal of a planetary Pax Americana also included a commitment to the spread of democratic and liberal values. Like any other empire, the American global version needed a civilizing mission, as more than one neocon commentator frankly admitted. The noise about democratizing other regions, especially the Middle East, grew much louder following the failure to find any weapons of mass destruction in Iraq. But the truth about the neoconservatives was that their commitment to democracy abroad had never been firmly principled—as anyone who could remember their record during the Reagan era would find difficult to deny.

Those were the years of the neoconservative ascendancy, when the founding generation, including former Trotskyists (or worse, former Democrats) entered the Republican Party and began to displace the traditional Goldwater conservatives. While many in the next generation—including Wolfowitz, Kristol, Perle, and Abrams—were rewarded with important positions in the Reagan and Bush administrations, the most prominent and vocal spokeswoman for neoconservative foreign policy was U.S. ambassador to the United Nations Jeane J. Kirkpatrick. Her only lasting contribution to political philosophy was to distinguish between authoritarian and totalitarian regimes, an argument that permitted the United States to provide financial and military support to some of the most vicious dictatorships around the world because their leaders supported the West against communism.

During those final years of the Soviet empire, the neoconservatives denounced Western proponents of human rights and democracy as naïve at best and Communist fellow travelers at worst. Foreshadowing dark events to come two decades hence, Kirkpatrick openly endorsed the military dictators who were later found to have run Argentina's "dirty war" of murder and torture against leftists and liberals.

As others have observed, the former Communists of the American neoconservative movement had changed their ideology but not their character. Torture, disappearances, and massacres were acceptable then; deception, illegal war, and torture are acceptable now. The end justified the means, and still does.

AT A DEEPER philosophical level, the neoconservatives appear to believe that, as the American writer Randolph Bourne once observed wryly, "War is the health of the state." That very few of them or their children would ever be called upon to actually fight and die may have accounted for their aggressive attitude.

The calamitous events of September 11 quickly amplified the usual drone of belligerent rhetoric from the far right into a deafening roar. The neoconservatives showed relatively little enthusiasm for the war in Afghanistan, where an internationally isolated Islamist government had afforded sanctuary to al Qaeda. Overthrowing the Taliban was certainly necessary—and enjoyed the support of NATO, the United Nations, and the entire civilized world—but didn't advance their agenda. Their real target was Iraq, and they began to prepare the way for invasion, both publicly and furtively behind closed doors.

Inside and outside government, the neoconservatives promoted a series of falsehoods to justify a policy of preemptive war that could later be extended to other enemy states. It has since become obvious that much so-called intelligence cited by the administration had no credibility, from the tales of mobile biowarfare labs peddled by an informant code-named Curveball to the forged documents claiming that Iraq had sought to obtain enriched uranium ore from Niger. It is indisputable that administration officials at the highest levels ignored credible evidence that contradicted their alarmist statements.

Over and over again the president, the vice president, the secretaries of defense and state, and the national security adviser grossly exaggerated the dangers posed by Iraq, invoking frightening images of a mushroom cloud and implying that the secular Iraqi regime was somehow connected with the Islamic extremist al Qaeda. Assisted by a credulous press corps and a battalion of columnists, editorial writers, war bloggers, and broadcast loudmouths—the "windbags of war"—they succeeded in convincing the American public that Saddam Hussein posed an imminent danger. When the Pentagon's "shock and awe" assault commenced on March 19, 2003, most Americans believed that Iraq already possessed nuclear weapons and was responsible for September 11. The catalogue of prevarications, fantasies, myths, misinterpreted reports, and ignored or discarded facts could fill volumes.

Early on, William Kristol, perhaps the most visible advocate for war in his roles as editor of the *Weekly Standard*, Fox News commentator, and chairman of the Project for the New American Century, had subtly hinted that truth alone might not always suffice. Making ready for war, he wrote in an October 2002 column for the *Washington Post*, would "require the president, at times, to mislead rather than to clarify, to deceive rather than to explain." The main target of these deceptions was Saddam himself, according to Kristol, but that would necessitate deceiving everyone else, too.

Kristol's prediction turned out to be correct, although not in a way that vindicates him—or Bush. Aside from the Bush administration's countless attempts to deceive and mislead Congress, the U.N. Security Council, the public, and the press, the president proposed a scheme designed to fool Saddam.

The notes of a secret meeting between the president and British prime minister Tony Blair on January 31, 2003, show that Bush wanted to lure the Iraqi dictator into a fatal error with a simple trick. Concerned that the U.N. weapons inspectors who had returned to Iraq were failing to find any hidden weapons that would justify the invasion scheduled for March, he told Blair that the United States might send "U-2 reconnaissance planes with fighter cover over Iraq, painted in UN colors . . . If Saddam fired on them, he would be in breach [of U.N. resolutions]." And despite the absence of any forbidden weapons, the Anglo-American coalition would seize the excuse to invade.

Risky and almost farcical, the plan to fly fake U.N. reconnaissance aircraft over Iraq must have been devised in the same spirit as that "well-planned series of deplorable 'incidents' on the Mexican border" mulled by the White House junta in *It Can't Happen Here*. Three years later, Bush's scheme to lure Iraq into an armed provocation was revealed on the front page of the *New York Times*. Neither the British nor the American government denied the story.

The Bush scheme, like all of the invented reasons for this "elective war," evoked another, much nastier parallel. It was too inflammatory to be mentioned by anyone except, oddly enough, a conservative columnist and former Reagan administration official writing in the *Washington Times*. Paul Craig Roberts warned that the "use of forged evidence opens Mr. Bush to unflattering comparisons that his enemies will not hesitate to make.

They will point out that it was Adolf Hitler's strategy to fabricate evidence in order to justify his invasion of a helpless country. He used S.S. troops dressed in Polish uniforms to fake an attack on the German radio station at Gleiwitz on Aug. 31, 1939. Following the faked attack, Hitler announced: 'This night for the first time Polish regular soldiers fired on our own territory.' As German troops poured into Poland, Hitler declared: 'The Polish state has refused the peaceful settlement of relations which I desired, and has appealed to arms.' The German High Command called the German invasion of Poland a counterattack."

TO IMPOSE PERMANENT war on a democratic society, deception is essential. Policy makers and their propagandists must always pretend to prefer peace, and must promise to wage war only as a last resort, as President Bush claimed to be doing in the months after he decided to invade Iraq. Not only was Iraq not invaded as a last resort, but the neoconservative authors of that war regarded the overthrow of Saddam Hussein as the opening chapter of a far wider and longer military campaign. While few of them actually enlist, especially in the present generation, they nevertheless seem to regard armed conflict as beneficial and necessary.

Not many politicians or pundits in Washington would be willing to articulate such belligerence with complete candor, however, for fear of sounding dangerous and possibly deranged. Still, there are a few who speak more frankly than they should. Among these is Michael Ledeen, a writer, scholar, and part-time intelligence operative, who blurts out what his comrades hesitate to say.

Unlike most of the academics, bureaucrats, officials, and journalists of his stripe, Ledeen is an adventurous troublemaker, which may explain his more confrontational style. Over the years his name has frequently surfaced in twilight intrigues and questionable circumstances, occasionally drawing the attention of prosecutors both here and in Italy, although he has never been charged with any wrongdoing. He has worked as a consultant at various times to the Pentagon, the State Department, and the National Security Council. Yet on more than one occasion, he has set up back-channel communications with foreign intelligence agencies, provoking the anger of U.S. officials.

While studying and working in Rome, he allegedly befriended some of the most disreputable characters on the Italian far right, including rogue intelligence agents and members of the notorious, secretive P-2 Masonic lodge that conspired against Italy's democratic government. At the same time, in the late 1970s, he is known to have advised SISMI, the Italian military intelligence service, on the subject of combating terrorism. His work for SISMI coincided with the period when fascist provocateurs tied to the intelligence agency and the P-2 lodge were perpetrating false-flag atrocities, including the bombing of the Bologna train station, that were attributed to the left. Ledeen has denied any involvement with P-2, and no evidence has ever emerged to link him to those conspiracies.

Two decades ago, after returning to Washington, Ledeen played a central role in the Iran-Contra affair that almost brought down the Reagan administration. Working with Lt. Col. Oliver North, he helped to arrange one of the first secret arms-for-hostages deals with Tehran through an Iranian arms dealer named Manucher Ghorbanifar. CIA officials later cut off Ghorbanifar after multiple polygraph tests showed him to be untrustworthy.

More recently, Ledeen has been suspected of involvement with the perpetrators of the Niger uranium forgeries, which reached the National Security Council via Italian intelligence agents and a reporter for *Panorama*, a Rome-based magazine that has employed Ledeen. (That publication also happens to be owned by his friend, the former prime minister and media mogul Silvio Berlusconi, whose electoral coalition included Italy's neofascist party.)

Ledeen vehemently denies any role in promoting the Niger forgeries. At the same time, he speaks proudly of his friendship with Ahmed Chalabi, the Iraqi National Congress politician who foisted so much fraudulent intelligence concerning Saddam Hussein's weapons of mass destruction on the Pentagon, the CIA, and major American news organizations. Ledeen has worked closely with the Pentagon's Office of Special Plans, the intelligence operation used by neoconservative officials in the Bush administration to circumvent the CIA and promote Chalabi's WMD tall tales, all of which have since been disproved.

Since September 11, 2001, the busy Ledeen has also renewed his connections with Ghorbanifar, in collaboration with the Office for Special Plans. Their aim has been to destabilize the regime in Tehran and seize control of Iran policy from the State Department, which they regard as too conciliatory. In addition to his own freqent consultations in Europe with Ghorbanifar, Ledeen set up a series of controversial meetings in Rome for the Iranian with American and Italian defense officials. Among the Pentagon employees attending at least one of those Rome meetings with Ghorbanifar in 2003 was Larry Franklin, an Iran expert who has since pleaded guilty to federal charges of unlawfully giving classified information to lobbyists for the American Israel Public Affairs Committee.

Precisely what Ledeen was trying to accomplish in his covert activities remains mysterious, but his broader aims are clear enough. Only days before American troops began their march to Baghdad, he predicted with evident relish that the coming conflict would quickly spread. "As soon as we land in Iraq, we're going to face the whole terrorist network, Iran, Iraq, Syria, and

Saudi Arabia are the big four, and then there's Libya." In an interview with journalist Robert Dreyfuss, he went further: "I think we're going to be obliged to fight a regional war, whether we want to or not. It may turn out to be a war to remake the world." He has called for total war, a term with terrible connotations of civilian carnage and merciless domination.

For Ledeen this ominous conflagration is to be anticipated, not avoided, because war will hasten the "creative destruction" of the traditional societies that are America's natural enemies. In his 2003 book, *The War Against the Terror Masters*, he portrayed a stark confrontation that can only be resolved with bloodshed. "They cannot feel secure so long as we are there, for our very existence—our existence, not our politics—threatens their legitimacy," he wrote. "They must attack us in order to survive, just as we must destroy them to advance our historic mission."

Shortly after the war began, he declared that Americans would not only be willing to sacrifice to pursue that mission, but that they would positively enjoy the bloodbath. "I think the level of casualties is secondary," he said at a briefing sponsored by the American Enterprise Institute. "I mean, it may sound like an odd thing to say, but all the great scholars who have studied American character have come to the conclusion that we are a warlike people and that we love war. . . . What we hate is not casualties, but losing."

His penchant for mass mayhem and the triumph of brute force can be traced to the very beginning of his strange career. As a young scholar of Italian fascism and a biographer of Gabriele d'Annunzio, the Fascist organizer and poet, Ledeen exhibited a peculiar admiration for the "creative destruction" embodied in that ideology (although he claimed to detest the actual regimes of Hitler and Mussolini). Among his early books was *Fascism: An Informal Introduction to Its Theory and Practice*

(1976), a volume coauthored with the late Renzo de Felice, a sympathetic historian of the Fascist movement in Italy. The controversial de Felice, who also wrote a seven-volume biography of Mussolini, argued that Fascism should be regarded as the legitimate political ideology of a rising European middle class.

Not surprisingly, Ledeen's rhetoric takes on a menacing tone when he is agitated. In a 1999 essay, he demanded the impeachment and removal of Bill Clinton, whom he considered a weak, unworthy, and corrupt man lacking the martial character of a true national leader. "New leaders with an iron will are required to root out the corruption and either reestablish a virtuous state, or to institute a new one . . . ," he warned. "If we bask in false security and drop our guard, the rot spreads, corrupting the entire society. Once that happens, only violent and extremely unpleasant methods can bring us back to virtue."

Those overheated passages may be found in a book he wrote to popularize the "iron rules" of leadership set down by Machiavelli, the Renaissance politician and essayist whose reputation Ledeen has tried to rehabilitate. Like his hero, who sought to advise the Medicis and Borgias, Ledeen valorizes war and scorns peace.

"Everlasting peace is a dream, not even a pleasant one; war is a necessary part of God's arrangement of the world," writes Ledeen, quoting a famous Prussian general with approval. "Without war the world would deteriorate into materialism." In this enthusiasm for blood and conquest, if nothing else, Ledeen resembles the Fascist leaders he studied, who worshipped war and aggression as the most important hallmarks of a great nation.

LEDEEN'S PECULIAR IDEAS and gamy background haven't prevented him from attaining a position of considerable influence in right-wing Washington. Perched in the Freedom Chair at the American Enterprise Institute, contributing regularly to the *National Review*, and consulting frequently with officials at the Pentagon and the White House, he is certainly a very senior neoconservative spokesman. The most important connection he has established is his informal status as an adviser to Karl Rove.

Only days before the invasion of Iraq, the *Washington Post* published a long list of people consulted regularly by Rove on policy and politics. Ledeen was the only foreign affairs adviser named in the article, whose main source was clearly the presidential adviser himself. Why they might connect should be obvious to anyone who knows the careers of both men. The enigmatic intelligence operative would no doubt fascinate the cunning political operative, renowned since his days as a young Nixon trickster. In attitude and ideology, they were well matched.

According to Ledeen, Rove had urged: "Anytime you have a good idea, tell me." More than once, he boasted, the ideas he has faxed to Rove have appeared in a directive or a speech. The ugly speech Rove delivered to the Conservative Party certainly echoed themes in Ledeen's writing—especially the insinuation that liberals and Democrats are soft on terror and that only Republicans possess the martial virtues necessary to defend America. But their agreement was more fundamental than that.

While Ledeen's absolutism and extremism place him outside the mainstream of American political traditions, his views converge neatly with the outlook of the late Leo Strauss, the University of Chicago political philosopher who became the patron saint of neoconservatism. A Jewish refugee from Hitler's Germany, the charismatic professor taught many of the figures who loom large in the Bush regime today, including former deputy secretary of defense Paul Wolfowitz and Abram Shulsky, the director of the Pentagon's Office of Special Plans, which was set up by Wolfowitz and Rumsfeld to find so-called intelligence supporting their war plan for Iraq. His influence extends to many others, notably including William Kristol, through students who became teachers in turn, such as Harvard's Harvey Mansfield and the late Allan Bloom of Chicago. His cultish influence on his followers was so strong that they still refer to themselves and each other as Straussians.

If only to reveal the authoritarian and militaristic strains in neoconservatism, the thinking of Strauss deserves examination.

More than thirty years after his death in 1973, his name is far more widely known and more controversial than at any time during his life. His acolytes are sometimes accused of fomenting a neoconservative political conspiracy, occasionally in blatantly anti-Semitic language. He is suspected of concealing his true ideas behind an intentional literary opacity. That is precisely what Strauss claimed the most important philosophers of history had done, carefully hiding their "esoteric" message within "exoteric" prose to avoid the dire consequences of honesty. (With respect to Plato, Socrates, Maimonides, and others to whom Strauss attributes such behavior, it should be said, his theory is widely dismissed as crankery.)

Like Machiavelli, Strauss viewed deception as the norm in both politics and philosophy. Only the select few would ever be initiated into the hidden truths.

Shadia Drury, a Canadian political scientist who has studied Strauss and his followers, notes the congruence of his ideas and those of Machiavelli. The supremely cynical author of *The Prince*, writes Drury, was "a theorist who was much admired by Strauss for everything except his lack of subtlety. Strauss endorsed Machiavellian tactics in politics—not just lies and the manipulation of public opinion but every manner of unscrupulous conduct necessary to keep the masses in a state of heightened alert, afraid for their lives and their families and therefore willing to do whatever was deemed necessary for the security of the nation. For Strauss as for Machiavelli, only the constant threat of a common enemy could save a people from becoming soft, pampered, and depraved."

Alan Gilbert, a professor of political science and international studies at the University of Denver (and former graduate adviser to Condoleezza Rice), has studied Strauss's relationships with the philosopher Martin Heidegger and the lawyer and professor Carl Schmitt. Heidegger and Schmitt joined the Nazi Party after Strauss left Germany in 1932; their Nazism and anti-Semitism disturbed Strauss, who otherwise admired both men. "But Strauss remains mesmerized by Heidegger's and Schmitt's politics," according to Gilbert, "particularly their anti-cosmopolitanism, their hatred for international peace, their love of militarism and war. His core political beliefs seem to have frozen in the late 1920s in a way that no subsequent experience would markedly affect."

Gilbert cites a letter Strauss sent to Schmitt in 1932, not long before Schmitt rose to become the principal legal theorist of the Nazi regime. (Schmitt believed that Strauss had written the most penetrating review of his theoretical work, *The Concept of the Political*, which defined politics as the struggle of one group to subdue others.) "The ultimate foundation of the Right is the principle of the natural evil of man; because man is by nature evil, he therefore needs *dominion*," wrote Strauss.

The most startling expression of Strauss's moral confusion during that period came in a letter he sent to a Jewish friend in May 1933 about the problem posed by the rise of Hitler and Nazis. "Just because the Germany of the Right does not tolerate us [Jews], it simply does not follow that the principles of the right are therefore to be rejected," wrote Strauss. "On the contrary, only on the basis of the principles of the right—fascist, authoritarian, *imperial*—is it possible in a dignified manner, without the ridiculous and pitiful appeal to 'the inalienable rights of man,' to protest against the mean nonentity [Hitler]."

Obviously a letter written more than seventy years ago by a

professor who is now deceased doesn't mean that today's neo-conservatives are secret fascists. But given their cultish venera-tion of its author, that appalling letter does place their militarist enthusiasms and imperial ambitions in a context that contrasts sharply with their supposed crusade for democracy.

It seems quite possible that, like Machiavelli, the great icon Strauss—and after him, Ledeen and leading contemporary neoconservatives—believed that people are fundamentally evil, that they must be ruled firmly from above, and that perpetual war is the inevitable condition of humanity. Could that be the hidden teaching behind the public rhetoric about democracy and freedom?

ALTHOUGH THE NEOCONSERVATIVES have proved adept in developing magazines, journals, foundations, think tanks, and a wide variety of other institutions, not to mention ideas and ideologies, they have never demonstrated a great talent for democratic politics. Among their frustrated ob-jectives, for instance, is to subvert the liberalism of American Jews and herd them into the Republican Party. Yet despite their control of important Jewish publications and the disproportion-ate visibility they enjoy in the mainstream media, that little proj-ect has been a dismal failure. Elections come and go, and Jewish voters continue to support liberal ideals and Democratic candidates with a consistency that is surpassed only by African Americans. The majority of the Jewish community was ahead of the rest of the nation in rejecting the Iraq war as early as 2003, according to public opinion polls—a blunt rejection of the neo-conservative agenda.

More broadly, the neoconservatives have been unable to de-velop a significant national political base, and their plans for perpetual war, if presented candidly, would be very unlikely to attract such a following. What they have done instead over the past two decades is to cultivate an alliance with the religious right. At first glance this combination might seem unlikely and even bizarre. How could an elite of secular (and largely Jewish) Eastern urban intellectuals join forces with fundamentalist Christian ministers from the South? But over the past twenty years, as neoconservative ideologues ascended in the national security establishment, and the leaders of the religious right have risen in the Republican Party, they have indeed combined to create a powerful and aggressive coalition.

This convergence of neocons and "theocons" has been continuous, successful, and increasingly tight during the Bush administration. It is not unusual—to take just one small example—for Pat Robertson's television show, *The 700 Club*, to feature Michael Ledeen talking about the urgent necessity to expand the war from Iraq to Iran. In right-wing media and institutions as well as in government, evangelical Christians and secular neoconservatives collaborate regularly.

THE MOST FATEFUL collaborations between neoconservatives and evangelicals have occurred behind closed doors, under heavy classification, at the uppermost levels of the Pentagon. That is where Rumsfeld brought together his own most trusted deputy, Stephen Cambone, with Lt. Gen. William G. "Jerry" Boykin to create an elite defense intelligence operation. Rumsfeld named Cambone to the newly created position of under secretary of defense for intelligence, and appointed Boykin as his deputy.

Once described as Rumsfeld's hatchetman, Cambone is a perfect Straussian neoconservative, trained in one of the academic cult's favored redoubts at Claremont College in California. Boykin is a dedicated spiritual warrior of the religious right, whose flamboyant public statements created a severe embarrassment for the White House not long after his Pentagon appointment. Journalist William Arkin reported on speeches that Boykin had been delivering in churches around the country, recounting his battles against Muslim warlords in Somalia and explaining that the war on terror is truly a crusade against the Antichrist.

"Satan wants to destroy this nation, he wants to destroy us as a nation, and he wants to destroy us as a Christian army," the general informed a rapt congregation in Oregon. America's enemies, he continued, "will only be defeated if we come against them in the name of Jesus."

Speaking at a Baptist church in Oklahoma, Boykin displayed the photographs he had taken while serving in Somalia in 1993, not long after the ill-fated *Blackhawk Down* helicopter crash that resulted in the killing of a dozen American soldiers. One of those photos showed a "strange dark mark" that appeared to hover over the Somali capital of Mogadishu.

"Ladies and gentleman, this is your enemy," he told the congregation as he displayed the photo on a screen. "It is the principalities of darkness. . . . It is a demonic presence in that city that God revealed to me as the enemy." Battling the Muslim warlord who ruled Mogadishu, said Boykin, he suffered a crisis of faith. Then he realized that his religious faith made him superior to his foe. "I knew that my god was bigger than his," recalled Boykin. "I knew that my god was a real God and his was an idol."

Those last remarks were taken as an inflammatory slur against Islam, sparking demands for Boykin's firing. He apologized instead, and Rumsfeld blithely ignored demands that he dismiss the erratic general. "We're a free people," said the defense secretary.

By the spring of 2006, Cambone and Boykin had been implicated, along with their boss, in the policies that contributed to the ever-widening scandal of detainee torture and abuse first exposed at Abu Ghraib prison. They had been overseeing super-secret "special access projects" of military intelligence that allegedly employed brutal interrogation techniques. Cambone had allegedly authorized interrogation techniques in Iraq that violated the Geneva conventions. Nothing was done to discipline them. Neither Boykin, an admired friend of the most powerful figures on the religious right, including James Dobson, Pat Robertson, and Southern Baptist Convention leader Bobby Welch, nor Cambone, the favorite of the once-invulnerable Rumsfeld, could be touched.

KEEPING SUCH CLOSE quarters with religious zealots can be challenging for secular intellectuals, as the Canadian Jewish speechwriter David Frum found out when he realized that "everyone" was expected to attend the daily Christian prayer meetings in the Bush White House. But culture clashes are the exception, not the rule. Over time, the neocons have willingly acceded to fundamentalist orthodoxy on issues ranging from abortion and stem-cell research to creationism.

As long ago as 1986, Irving Kristol shocked readers of the *New York Times* when he published an essay in that newspaper taking the side of Christian fundamentalists against the teaching of evolution. Known as the supremely influential godfather of neoconservatism, Kristol marked an intellectual (or anti-intellectual) watershed with repeated, intemperate denunciations of secular humanism. Over time, such pandering to the Christian fundamentalists became less and less surprising. Even recurrent anti-Semitism among leaders on the religious right could be excused—and often was—in order to sustain the strategic coalition.

What kept them together, consistently, was agreement on the

question of Israel. Neoconservatives and fundamentalists alike support the Likud Party's maximalist conception of a Greater Israel, which meant the annexation of occupied Arab territory, including East Jerusalem, and the refusal to negotiate the establishment of a viable, independent Palestinian homeland. The Christian Zionists of the religious right are much more fervent and implacable in their Zionism than most American Jews, who prefer a negotiated land for peace settlement.

Fundamentalist support for Israel is based on apocalyptic biblical prophecy, of course, rather than concern about the fate of the Jewish people. According to popular interpretations of the book of Revelation, the return of God's chosen to the Holy Land is a precondition for Armageddon, the final confrontation between Jesus Christ and the Antichrist. The Jews will either convert or be swallowed by a lake of fire—along with all the other bad people on Earth—while the remnant of faithful Christians will be saved to rule the world for a thousand years at the side of Jesus himself.

This entertaining eschatological narrative—featured daily on Christian television networks to help separate the rubes from their money—troubles the neoconservatives not at all. They are in no position to criticize militant superstition, having long since discarded liberal rationalism and enlightened pluralism to march with the religious right. Although they are atheists and agnostics—"nonobservant" as Irving Kristol once said of himself—they advocate the cultivation of fervent religious belief in society. The high-minded justification for this cynical approach can be found in the writings of Strauss and Machiavelli.

Robert Locke, a conservative and former editor of the right-wing Web site Frontpagemag.com who studied under Strauss at the University of Chicago, described the late professor as an atheist and elitist "who believed that religion was the great necessity for ordinary men." For Strauss, only the strictest faith could inculcate the fear and obedience needed to prevent nations from descending into materialism, indulgence, sloth, and corruption.

Ledeen derives the same essential message from Machiavelli. In an orderly state, the people accept the law and the sovereign as divinely ordained. Interpreting Machiavelli (and Strauss indirectly as well), he discussed religion's central role in the Florentine's "iron rules of leadership" at the American Enterprise Institute. As "the first spin doctor," Machiavelli understood that "the people had to believe in the noble qualities of their leaders" if only to ensure their willingness to "die for the good of the state." Inspiring and motivating modern armies "can best be accomplished by the effective use of religion." (Aristotle reached a similar conclusion about eighteen hundred years earlier, when he observed, "A tyrant must put on the appearance of uncommon devotion to religion." So did Karl Marx, for that matter.)

In Ledeen's estimation, "American evangelical Christianity is the sort of 'good religion' Machiavelli calls for. The evangelicals do not quietly accept their destiny, believing instead they are called upon to fight corruption and reestablish virtue." Specifically, many conservative evangelicals fervently believe that fighting corruption and reestablishing virtue quite literally requires "taking dominion" over civil government in the United States—and eventually winning the entire planet for Christ. They reject the constitutional separation of church and state as a myth propagated by secular humanists. They uphold the United States as a Christian nation that must be ruled by godly men according to biblical principles—which sanction debt slavery and the death penalty for homosexuals, adulterers, and disobedient children.

As Ledeen suggested, many evangelicals believe that the Almighty ordained the Bush presidency. Such notions gained currency in the wake of September 11. General Boykin has lectured on the topic, noting that the president actually entered the Oval Office despite the expressed will of the people in 2000. "George Bush was not elected by a majority of the voters in the U.S.," said Boykin. "He was appointed by God." Ralph Reed, the former director of the Christian Coalition (and disgraced associate of convicted lobbyist Jack Abramoff), suggested that God selected the president because "He knew George Bush had the ability to lead in this compelling way." Nor was this revelation confined solely to Protestants. Former New York mayor Rudolph Giuliani, a devout but not excessively rigorous Catholic, announced his own opinion that "there was some divine guidance in the President being elected."

For his part, Bush continues to encourage this very flattering idea. He told journalist Bob Woodward that rather than seek the counsel of his own father, a former president, he consulted "a higher father" to prepare for war. In 2005, he confided to Palestinian leaders Nabil Shaath and Mahmoud Abbas that the Lord was in charge of Mideast policy. "I'm driven with a mission from God," he told the astonished pair. "God would tell me, 'George, go and fight those terrorists in Afghanistan.' And I did, and then God would tell me, 'George, go and end the tyranny in Iraq,' and I did."

WILL GOD INSTRUCT Bush to bomb Iran before his term in office ends?

As the war in Iraq festered with no end in sight, and the president's approval numbers sank into that desert sand, the neoconservatives and the religious rightists seemed to be turning again toward war. During the first months of 2006, four years after Rove beat the war drums to win more seats in the House and Senate, whispers began to circulate that the only way to preserve Republican power and the Bush presidency would be to take action against the Shiite Islamist regime in Teheran.

With each fresh warning from the White House, the Pentagon, and the State Department about the danger posed by Iran's nuclear program, with every rumor of American or Israeli plans to attack the Iranian nuclear facilities, suspicion grew that Bush planned to exploit the traditional rally effect of an expanded war. The sense of déjà vu intensified as the same themes and exaggerations used to demonize Iraq were shifted to Iran. The radical president of Iran, Mahmoud Ahmadinejad, speaks loudly of his antipathy to Israel and Jews, and as with Saddam Hussein, he was compared to Hitler. The American intelligence community, deprived of any diplomatic access to Iran for the past quarter-century, was forced to rely on dubious information from émigré groups and potential fabricators, much the same as when it tried to assess Iraqi weapons and intentions.

Despite fears that Bush would take political advantage of the situation, he flinched from action against Iran before the midterm election. Instead he sought to warn voters, in language similar to Rove's most inflammatory speeches, that voting for Democrats was the same as voting for terrorism. At a campaign event in Georgia the week before Election Day, he said: "However they put it, the Democrat approach in Iraq comes down to this: The terrorists win and America loses."

The impulse toward a wider war remains powerful on the right, despite the midterm electoral setback for Republicans. Both in Washington and in the American heartland, the same forces once eager to wage war on Iraq were agitating for action against Iran—including the neoconservatives, especially Michael Ledeen, and the evangelical Christians. For Ledeen, who has been propagandizing for regime change in Tehran for years, the latest conflict created an opportunity to renew his clandestine activities with Manucher Ghorbanifar and the old Iran-Contra network. For the religious right, a looming confrontation with the mullahs held even greater prophetic meaning than the ouster of

Saddam. At Wal-Mart stores across the country, the bestselling book during the first months of 2006 was Rev. John Hagee's *Jerusalem Countdown,* which urged the United States to wage preventive war on Iran or suffer the wrath of God for failing to protect Israel. On nationwide television broadcasts and from the pulpit of his San Antonio megachurch, Hagee predicts that a military strike is coming, leading inexorably to Armageddon and the final battle when Jesus returns to destroy the forces of the Antichrist.

The difference between Iraq and Iran is that the mullahs in Tehran truly could pose a threat to world peace if and when they can produce nuclear warheads, which their scientists may well be trying to accomplish. If they can be discouraged by a combination of warnings, sanctions, and diplomacy, perhaps the distant but disturbing prospect of a nuclear Iran can be prevented. The problem is that no matter how much bluster emanates from the White House and the Pentagon, Bush's war in Iraq has weakened the United States politically, militarily, diplomatically, and economically. Having spent so much blood and treasure on a false problem, our government is much less capable of dealing with a real one.

But opening another front in the long war may still mobilize the dispirited right-wing base for the next electoral confrontation. Should Bush and Cheney eventually decide to extend hostilities into Iran, Syria, or Lebanon, their determination is not likely to be diminished by dissent in Congress.

TWO

LAWLESSNESS AND ORDER

The loss of liberty at home is to be charged to the provisions against danger, real or imagined, from abroad.

—JAMES MADISON

He that would make his own liberty secure must guard even his enemy from oppression; for if he violates this duty he establishes a precedent that will reach to himself.

—THOMAS PAINE

HOW THE REPUBLICAN regime planned to govern domestically in permanent wartime first became clear when John Ashcroft, then the United States attorney general, appeared before the Senate Judiciary Committee three months after September 11. After passing the USA Patriot Act with little debate or deliberation at Ashcroft's behest, leading senators were alarmed to learn that the Bush administration had other, even more radical plans to curtail civil liberties that neither he nor Ashcroft had bothered to mention earlier. Three weeks after the passage and signing of the Patriot Act, the president had signed a sweeping executive order authorizing the use of military tribunals to convict and execute any foreign national suspected of aiding or abetting terrorism.

Under Bush's order, all traditions of American jurisprudence and all rights normally afforded criminal defendants under the Bill of Rights and by statute were to be abrogated at his command—without so much as a nod to Congress or the courts. Whether in the United States, in other countries, or on naval vessels at sea, these military trials would be held in complete secrecy. Evidence inadmissible at any normal trial in a civilized country could be introduced, and much of the evidence would be withheld from the defendant because of its classified nature. Conviction would not require proof beyond a reasonable doubt. Panels of military officers would render the verdicts, which would not be subject to appeal. Only two out of three judges would need to agree in order to impose a death sentence.

The defendants would not be able to choose their counsel, of course, and they would have no access to American courts.

In other words, the president had arrogated to himself the right to order phony trials that concluded with summary executions. "We are letting George W. Bush get away with the replacement of the American rule of law with military kangaroo courts," roared William Safire in the *New York Times*, who denounced the tribunals as "a Soviet-style abomination."

For three weeks, the worried senators were unable to induce Ashcroft to come up to the Capitol to discuss the administration's constitutional trespasses. The promises of cooperation and consultation he had made the previous spring, during his difficult Senate confirmation proceedings, were no longer operative.

It should have been obvious by then that neither the president nor the attorney general cared much whether Congress approved of their actions. Indeed, Ashcroft hinted at the new imbalance of power eight days after 9/11, when his aides delivered the draft of the USA Patriot Act to Capitol Hill. The bill's name crudely implied that anyone questioning its sweeping provisions was skirting treason. Who would vote against the USA? Who opposed patriotism? Anyone who questioned the tough provisions of the Patriot Act would be defined politically as soft on terrorism. As Senator Robert Byrd of West Virginia later recalled, while admitting that he regretted having voted yea on the Patriot Act, the Republican leadership had bulldozed the bill across Capitol Hill so swiftly that his colleagues in both Houses had almost no time to read the 300-plus pages, let alone analyze the legal meaning of their content.

Perhaps even to insist on reading the entire document before voting aye would have been deemed a sign of deficient loyalty. That was the implication when Ashcroft demanded that Congress pass the Patriot Act within days after he sent it up to Capitol Hill.

As a former United States senator from Missouri, John Ashcroft was familiar with the Senate's processes. Arguably, he may even have understood the purpose of those processes, as conceived by the nation's founders, namely to forestall abrupt, intemperate, misguided, and dangerous acts of government. The Senate's deliberative function—the authority delegated by the Constitution to every senator to require as much time as necessary for thought and discussion—was designed by the framers to block the hasty passage of bad legislation.

So there was considerable irony when Ashcroft—like many conservative lawyers, a self-styled defender of the "original intent" of the Constitution's authors—quickly discarded the great document's framework for legislative action. The foundation of a democratic republic is the process followed in making and executing laws. Undoing that process in the name of security is the first step toward authoritarian lawlessness.

Although Ashcroft's impatience for action was understandable, there was irony in his sudden zeal, too. On taking over as attorney general, he had shrugged off warnings about the terrorist threat in favor of a narrow, moralistic agenda. He had wanted to prosecute providers of medical marijuana and doctors in Oregon who assisted the suicides of terminally ill patients. He had especially wanted to prosecute pornographers.

When FBI director Louis Freeh approached the attorney general to request additional resources to fight terrorism, months before 9/11, he had brushed the request aside. (Freeh soon resigned.) Ashcroft's first budget—submitted to the White House on the day before the Twin Towers fell—had sought new spending on sixty-eight programs, none related to counterterrorism. He had rejected the FBI's request to hire hundreds of new field agents, translators, and intelligence analysts to detect foreign terror threats. He had proposed to cut $65 million from a Clinton-era program that aided state and local authorities to prepare for terrorist attacks. Those errors were wholly typical of the early Bush administration, which, despite many warnings about the threat from al Qaeda, had other priorities.

The catastrophe altered Ashcroft's priorities but not his arrogance. He ordered the Patriot Act to be drafted without even pretending to consult Congress. That assignment fell to a group of Justice Department attorneys led by Viet Dinh, the assistant attorney general for legal policy, and Michael Chertoff, the assistant attorney in charge of the criminal division and future secretary of homeland security. Working closely with them was a bright, ambitious young lawyer named John Yoo in the department's Office of Legal Counsel.

Like many other Bush appointees in the Justice Department, the office of White House counsel, and the federal judiciary, Dinh and Chertoff both were stalwarts of the powerful right-wing legal network known as the Federalist Society. They had served together as lawyers on the Senate Whitewater Committee, where they spearheaded the Republicans' unabashedly partisan probe of the Clintons' personal investments. Yoo was also active in the Federalist Society and had won one of the society's highest awards before Ashcroft hired him.

The Bush lawyers worked with great industry and dispatch. Their team completed a draft of the Patriot Act within days, partly because the bill contained little that was new or original. Reading through its provisions, legal experts observed that it was largely a patchwork of the department's previously frustrated attempts to expand executive power. While many provisions of the act simply codified existing powers of government to investigate and prosecute suspected terrorists, certain sections severely weakened traditional Fourth Amendment protections.

The most controversial provisions gave the government unprecedented authority to search the records and premises of citizens without seeking the consent of a judge, so long as the purpose supposedly concerned terrorism or foreign intelligence—and in some instances even without that assurance.

Section 215 authorized the FBI to secretly conduct wide-ranging searches of the records of American citizens—anything from credit card charges and bank withdrawals to video rental receipts and, infamously, library slips—without judicial warrants or oversight. The citizen whose records are thus invaded need not be a terror suspect, while those who turn over the records are forbidden to disclose the search to anyone.

Section 218 expanded the authority granted to federal agencies under the Foreign Intelligence Surveillance Act of 1978, which had been carefully designed, only in national security cases, to relieve the normal requirements for a search, including a warrant and probable cause to believe that a crime had been committed. Under the 1978 law, the Foreign Intelligence Surveillance Court, whose proceedings are secret and include only lawyers for the government, would be required to authorize secret searches (known as "sneak and peek") of anyone, so long as "the primary purpose" of the search involved foreign intelligence. The Patriot Act permitted those same intrusions if gathering foreign intelligence was merely "a purpose" of the surveillance. The same section also permitted roving wiretaps of any phone or computer that the targeted person might use—again without any guarantee that the target is a terror suspect.

Section 213 permitted black-bag entry into a private home, and the placement of surveillance chips in a home computer, without even the fig leaf of a foreign intelligence investigation. Federal agents could return surreptitiously to the same premises repeatedly, without informing the residents that their home had been invaded.

Those became the most notorious changes, but there were more. With few safeguards and little accountability, the Patriot Act severely curtailed the protections of the Fourth Amendment against unreasonable search and seizure of a person's property. With no evidence of wrongdoing, the government could subject law-abiding citizens to the same secret invasions once reserved for suspected spies and felons.

As Lincoln Caplan, the former editor of Yale Law School's *Legal Affairs*, observed: "What is more startling than the scope of these new powers is that the government can use them on people who aren't suspected of committing a crime. Innocent people can be deprived of any clue that they are being watched and that they may need to defend themselves."

Upon delivering his extraordinary handiwork to Congress, with the nation still reeling, Ashcroft called for instantaneous passage. He had little patience with the people's elected representatives and their need to consider a bill with hundreds of pages and dozens of complex titles and sections. A day of hearings each in the House and the Senate should be sufficient. Appointed by a president who had lost the popular vote and entered office with his political legitimacy in doubt, the attorney general might have behaved less brusquely. But his style was perfectly consistent with the bill's substance, and the sweeping arrogation of power that was to follow in its wake.

Passage of the Patriot Act ultimately required a few weeks rather than a few days. In a process tainted by the administration's utter disregard for democratic debate and deliberation, the Republican leadership rammed the bill through Congress with few changes. The Senate's civil libertarians managed to delete a handful of absurdly egregious provisions. For example, Ashcroft wanted prosecutors to be permitted to use evidence obtained from wiretaps in other countries against criminal defendants, even if the same kind of surveillance would be illegal in the United States. He also wanted the authority to freeze the assets of criminal defendants, even if those assets were unrelated to their alleged offenses, a power long sought by the Justice Department's criminal division. Those sections were dropped and several others were modified. On October 23, 2001, the USA Patriot Act passed both houses of Congress.

Several weeks later, the *New York Times* published a front-page story that raised startling questions about the political distortion of the Bush administration's counterterror program. The *Times* revealed that Ashcroft and Dinh had demonstrated great concern about the privacy of a certain small group of gun-owning foreigners—even as they were drawing up new laws to nullify everyone else's Fourth Amendment protections.

On September 16, just five days after the 9/11 attacks, the FBI and the Bureau of Alcohol, Tobacco and Firearms had sought authority to use the national instant-check database that monitors gun purchasers in their urgent investigation of terror suspects. Dinh refused to permit the agents any access to the instant-check computer files. Comparing the records of gun purchasers against the names of terror suspects, the assistant attorney general ruled, would represent an improper trespass of their privacy rights. According to Dinh, the privacy ruling applied even to detainees under arrest for immigration violations.

That bizarre ruling, upheld by Ashcroft and the White House despite public and press outrage after its exposure, raised grave doubts about the administration's motives. Dinh's decision was an obvious political sop to Republican allies in the National Rifle Association and the firearms industry, which feared stricter regulation to keep automatic weapons out of the hands of potential terrorists. Had federal agents found the name of even one bona fide terror suspect in the instant-check database, legislators might be forced to enact strong new gun laws. (An al Qaeda handbook later found in Afghanistan showed that the terrorists were well aware of how easily firearms can be purchased in the United States.)

The Justice Department's Office of Legal Counsel contradicted Dinh's opinion. Yet Ashcroft not only insisted that federal law didn't permit the use of gun-purchase records for counterterror investigations, but he also insisted that the law should not be changed. If the attorney general saw no compelling need to allow such basic and obvious counterterror measures, simply because they would anger the "patriotic" gun lobby, then why should the rest of the country be subjected to the extraordinary provisions of the Patriot Act?

In retrospect—considering what we have since learned about the Bush administration and its interpretation of the Constitution that its officials swore to uphold—the congressional decision to entrust the White House with enhanced power seems terribly naïve.

Politicians of both parties, rarely courageous even in easier times, found themselves paralyzed by the nation's apocalyptic mood. Except for Senator Russell Feingold, the Wisconsin Democrat who cast the only vote against the Patriot Act, they weren't prepared to stand up against Bush and Ashcroft—especially when the president's approval ratings were rocketing toward unanimity.

DURING THE WEEKS that followed the attacks, federal agents arrested and detained more than a thousand foreign nationals, mostly of Middle Eastern and South Asian origin, on immigration charges. Hundreds were jammed into jails in New York and New Jersey, where they were held virtually incommunicado, confined to crowded cells for twenty-three hours a day, and in some cases beaten by guards. Hundreds were subjected to secret deportation hearings. The mistreatment and denial of basic rights were closer to the standards of a backward police state than a modern democracy.

At Ashcroft's request, Bush also signed a controversial executive

order permitting agents to tap or eavesdrop on discussions between federal prisoners and their lawyers. From that point forward,
this abrogation of traditional attorney-client privilege would require no judicial warrant.

Some immigrant prisoners were held for up to eight months
without charges, and Ashcroft firmly believed that he could
hold them indefinitely, or as long as he suspected them of even
the most tenuous terrorist connections. He also refused to release the names of those being held, supposedly to protect their
privacy. Eventually, he announced indictments against about a
hundred of the detainees, although the charges were in most
cases minor violations. He claimed that the mass detention had
prevented additional terrorist attacks, but never produced any
credible evidence. None of the detainees was ever charged as a
terrorist, and few if any provided any useful information. When
the Justice Department's own inspector general finally issued a
strongly critical report on the domestic detainees in 2003, the
attorney general held a press conference where he replied, "We
make no apologies."

ON NOVEMBER 13, 2001, three weeks after signing the
Patriot Act, the president announced that he had issued an order
authorizing military trials for suspected terrorists—whether they
had been captured in the war against the Taliban in Afghanistan
or elsewhere, including on American soil. The Justice Department explained that the order was meant to prevent the disclosure
of classified information in a normal court proceeding, as well as
the potential threat of terrorist attacks in courtrooms.

The most obvious attraction of the military tribunal for Bush
was its simplicity: A defendant could be sentenced to death and
executed without the burden of a public trial, a right to appeal,
or the necessity of proving guilt beyond a reasonable doubt.

Bush's order provided only a vague notion of who might be subjected to this process, and what kind of "full and fair" proceedings the accused could expect.

Nobody in the White House or the Justice Department had bothered to consult Congress about this radical departure from constitutional norms. When worried Republicans and Democrats had the temerity to inquire about the details, Ashcroft brushed their questions aside. But eventually, under increasing criticism from the mainstream press, Senate Democrats, liberals, and libertarians, he reluctantly agreed to make a brief appearance at a Senate Judiciary Committee hearing in early December 2001. His testimony that morning opened with a boilerplate recitation of his department's strenuous efforts to thwart terror. He tried to make nice noises about cooperating with and informing Congress—up to a point—and the need to balance civil liberties and national security.

And then he responded to his critics with undisguised anger:

> We need honest, reasoned debate, and not fear-mongering. To those who pit Americans against immigrants and citizens against non-citizens, to those who scare peace-loving people with phantoms of lost liberty, my message is this: Your tactics only aid terrorists, for they erode our national unity and diminish our resolve. They give ammunition to America's enemies, and pause to America's friends. They encourage people of goodwill to remain silent in the face of evil.

Ashcroft's treason-baiting outburst led the news coverage of his testimony—and provoked a barrage of negative commentary that marred the rest of his tenure. Unnoticed in the furious reaction to those bullying lines was his closing peroration on the powers of the executive.

The most important thing to remember, he noted with just a

touch of condescension, was that the Constitution "vests the president with the extraordinary and sole authority, as commander-in-chief, to lead our nation in times of war." He didn't mention that within two weeks after September 11, John Yoo had sent a memo on that very topic, the first of a series, over to the White House. Its conclusion was that the president possessed inherent power to wage war, wherever he chose and in whatever fashion he deemed necessary—regardless of any limits delineated by Congress.

JOHN ASHCROFT WASN'T the president's first choice for attorney general, but his personality and ideology suited the Republican regime well in the aftermath of 9/11. Like Bush, his thinking reflected the fundamentalist mind-set, and he, too, was inclined to identify his temporal authority with the will of the Almighty.

Originally, Bush had wanted to name Marc Racicot, the governor of Montana, as his chief law enforcement officer. But the bright, telegenic Racicot, who had served as the Bush-Cheney campaign's chief legal spokesman in Florida during the disputed ballot count that followed the 2000 election, was considered insufficiently zealous in his commitment to their cause by certain influential figures in the right-wing religious leadership. (Among his sins was an endorsement of stronger hate-crime statutes after the murder of Matthew Shepard, a young gay man, in Wyoming.)

A report on Racicot's alleged ideological shortcomings circulated by Robert P. George, an influential and ultraconservative Princeton law professor, effectively killed his nomination. Within a few days, Bush announced instead that he had chosen Ashcroft, the reliable favorite of evangelical politicians such as Ralph Reed and Jerry Falwell. His powerful backers in the leadership of the religious right were delighted, for they had made one of their own insiders into the nation's most powerful law enforcement officer.

Ashcroft had won the support of many evangelical leaders for president in 2000, before he folded his campaign to back Bush. More significantly, he was a member of the Council for National Policy, the highly secretive and exclusive organization whose five hundred members serve as a central committee for the religious right (see chapter 4). Meeting three times annually, the CNP permits no press coverage of its activities and swears all of its members to absolute secrecy about its proceedings. In 1999, the group vetted Bush at a closed meeting in San Antonio. Although his speech was recorded, both the Bush campaign and the CNP refused to release a tape or transcript.

Nearly every important right-wing political figure—from Phyllis Schlafly and Tim LaHaye to Pat Robertson and James Dobson—participates in the CNP, which seeks to transform America into a "Christian nation." Its membership has been broad enough to include Republican elected officials such as Tom DeLay and extremists like Gary North, a minister whose notion of biblical morality mandates the death penalty for adulterers and homosexuals. What they all share, at the very least, is the desire to elevate "godly men" such as Bush and Ashcroft into positions of authority.

When Bush sent Ashcroft's name up to the evenly divided Senate for confirmation, there was cloakroom talk of a filibuster—a remarkable fact considering that former senators are usually confirmed with little trouble. The vote to confirm him was exceptionally close.

Although Ashcroft's positions on abortion and civil rights were much debated, the most telling aspect of his Senate record was his overweening desire to change the Constitution. During his single six-year term, he sponsored no fewer than eleven constitutional amendments. (Only seventeen amendments have been ratified since the approval of the Bill of Rights in 1789.) His most irresponsible and sinister notion of "improvement" would have made the process of amending the Constitution far easier. Other amendments that he proposed included a bid to overturn the *Roe v. Wade* decision; a "human life amendment" to forbid some forms of contraception; an amendment to permit prayer in public schools; and another outlawing desecration of the American flag. Speaking at the National Religious Broadcasters convention as attorney general, he hinted that the Constitution is of secondary importance. "We are a nation called to defend freedom—a freedom that is not the grant of any government or document but is our endowment from God."

Ashcroft's sense of his biblical mission in government is captured in a ceremony that he repeated every time he prepared to take an oath for public office. The devout son and grandson of Pentecostal preachers, he would kneel down, like the Old Testament kings of Israel, to have his head anointed with holy oil by his aging dad. On the night before he was sworn in to the U.S. Senate, he and his father realized that they had no oil.

"Let's see if there's something in the kitchen," said the elder Ashcroft.

Moments later John Ashcroft was kneeling again, as he listened to his father's solemn voice and felt the slightly greasy fingers touching his temples. (Someone had found a bottle of Crisco oil.) His father passed away before he was sworn in as attorney general. On that occasion, he asked Supreme Court Justice Clarence Thomas to anoint him.

For an American elected official to mimic the ritual of the ancient Hebrew kings seemed almost blasphemous. Aside from its ostentatious piety, the anointment ceremony implied an authority derived from God. If that was what Ashcroft intended by this gesture, it would have been consistent with the theocratic dominion ideology of many of the religious rightists in the Council for National Policy.

Two years before 9/11, in commencement remarks delivered at Bob Jones University in 1999, Ashcroft had alluded to those beliefs. If his comprehension of American and world history was dim, his fervor could not be doubted. "Unique among the nations, America recognized the source of our character as being godly and eternal, not being civic and temporal," he said. "And because we have understood that our source is eternal, America has been different. We have no king but Jesus." (After he returned to private life in 2005, Ashcroft joined the law faculty at Pat Robertson's Regent University, an institution whose name the televangelist once explained as follows: "A regent is one who governs in the absence of a sovereign. . . . Someday we will rule and reign along with our sovereign, Jesus Christ.")

Ashcroft brought his own theocratic style into the Justice Department, where he held a daily prayer meeting. But the high-level aides who shaped legal policy in the Bush administration—notably Viet Dinh and John Yoo—were recruited through the more ecumenical right-wing network known as the Federalist Society. Heavily funded by the same conservative foundations that have built the right's broad intellectual infrastructure of think tanks, advocacy groups, media outlets, and training institutes over the past three decades, the society may be the single most successful and powerful project created by those sponsors. Less than twenty-five years after its founding by a handful of disgruntled conservative law students, the society now competes for influence among judges and law professors with the American Bar Association.

Actually, the society wields more clout in the federal judiciary than the ABA, and its prestige has only increased with the growing prevalence of Republican-appointed judges. Its leaders in Washington provided most of the legal muscle that so relentlessly pursued the Clintons in court and in Congress, including the former independent counsel Kenneth Starr and former solicitor general Ted Olson. Members of this clique occasionally joke that the Federalist Society is the true "vast right-wing conspiracy." They aren't really kidding.

For public relations purposes, Federalist Society officials and spokesmen insist that it has no ideological goals, and exists solely to encourage "debate on legal and public policy issues." It is fair to say that the society's membership is divided among libertarians, secular conservatives, and religious right-wingers. But the religious right wields enormous influence within the society, whose leadership overlaps with the Council for National Policy. The directors of the Federalist Society include CNP vice president T. Kenneth Cribb Jr., a former Reagan White House official, and Eugene Meyer, the society's longtime executive director, who has been listed as a CNP member. Donald P. Hodel, the former Reagan energy secretary and Christian Coalition president who now presides over the CNP, is a member of the Federalist Society's advisory board. And until recently, the society's religious liberty "practice group" was chaired by law professor Robert P. George. Both U.S. Chief Justice John G. Roberts and Justice Samuel Alito have been identified as Federalist members, although Roberts denied joining. The membership list is secret.

The society's political tilt is easily detected by examining its recommended reading list for students. The dominant names include Supreme Court Justice Antonin Scalia; Robert Bork, the former solicitor general rejected by the Senate when Ronald Reagan nominated him to the Supreme Court; and University of Texas law professor Lino Graglia, who describes himself as "far right" and is best known for publicly denigrating the "culture" of black and Hispanic students. Their outlook could hardly be described as libertarian.

At the heart of the Federalist Society's project lie a pair of related objectives: to roll back the Supreme Court precedents and government programs of the Great Society, the New Deal, and the Progressive Era, and to promote the originalist interpretation of the Constitution, which would nullify many of the laws and rights taken for granted by Americans. For the most fervent Federalist ideologues, the golden age was the Gilded Age, when business titans ruled without challenge. The primacy of property rights—not civil liberties, civil rights, or human rights— unites every faction among the Federalists.

In a sense, however, the Federalist Society's purpose is less to promote any particular line than to recruit and vet young partisan lawyers willing to do whatever may be necessary to advance the Republican regime. The outstanding example is the society's idol, Scalia, who hastily abandoned his lifelong devotion to originalist theory and states' rights in December 2000 to promote Republican rule in the ridiculous *Bush v. Gore* decision.

Ideology and argumentation can shift whenever required by expedience. What matters is the willingness to serve and expand power, as exemplified by the career of John Yoo.

ALTHOUGH YOO POSSESSED a middling title— deputy assistant attorney general—he created an intellectual framework for the new paradigm of unchecked executive authority adopted by his superiors, including Ashcroft, Cheney, Rumsfeld, and Bush. The practical meaning of Yoo's theory, developed in a series of classified legal memoranda, was that the president has inherent constitutional authority to ignore statutes and treaties approved by irritating congressional majorities and decisions handed down by meddling federal judges.

At the request of the White House, Yoo began to elucidate

his theory of an untrammeled presidency within days after 9/11. To prevent or deter terrorist acts on American soil, Yoo wrote, the president possessed tremendous latitude. If he believed that troops had to be deployed to defend against domestic attacks, the memo suggested, then he could also effectively suspend the Fourth Amendment, which ordinarily prevents government from depriving anyone of life, liberty, property, or privacy without probable cause to suspect criminal activity. Under certain conditions, the Fourth Amendment "should be no more relevant than it would be in cases of invasion or insurrection."

According to Yoo, the president's plenary power extended far beyond the specific authorization voted by Congress following 9/11. While the Authorization to Use Military Force underwrote his authority, it did not limit him. No statute could restrict his power to take whatever action he deemed necessary, against any individual or group, anywhere in the world. As Bradford Berenson, then an associate White House counsel, later told the *New York Times*, "Legally, the watchword became 'forward-leaning' by which everybody meant: 'We want to be aggressive. We want to take risks.' "

As the United States established detention facilities in Afghanistan and Guantánamo for prisoners captured during the war against the Taliban, a new question arose. What laws governed the imprisonment and interrogation of these prisoners? The legal arguments that justified the Bush administration's undermining of the Geneva Conventions can be traced to crucial memoranda authored by Yoo that encouraged the Pentagon and the White House to deny traditional protections to prisoners of war and detainees.

Bush administration policy makers and attorneys feared that the collection of useful intelligence would be severely hampered by the Geneva Conventions and other restrictions on the use of coercive interrogation. Although the original targets of Yoo's legal memos were the accused Taliban and al Qaeda prisoners in Guantánamo and Afghanistan, those same arguments and attitudes promoted tolerance of the brutal, coercive, and illegal interrogation methods that were later exposed in Iraq.

Douglas Feith, a leading neoconservative ideologue who served as under secretary of defense for policy, initially asked the military's Judge Advocate General Corps to devise policies that evaded or diluted the Geneva protections. But ranking JAG officers, who prided themselves on upholding traditional human rights safeguards, strongly opposed the changes that Feith and Rumsfeld wanted. Feith then turned to the Justice Department, where Yoo was assigned to formulate those arguments.

Yoo's key memorandum on the Geneva Conventions, dated January 9, 2002, argued that they should not be applied to prisoners captured in Afghanistan because the Taliban and al Qaeda had systematically violated the laws of war. Above and beyond those particulars, however, was Yoo's firm conviction that the president need not obey treaties and conventions that hindered him as commander in chief.

The memo was circulated to Ashcroft, White House counsel Alberto Gonzales, Cheney's counsel David Addington, and Defense Department general counsel William J. Haynes. Only the State Department, which Cheney and Rumsfeld had unsuccessfully sought to exclude from their deliberations, offered any negative comment on Yoo's "bold" departure. In a memo to Yoo disputing his conclusions, the department's chief counsel, William Howard Taft IV, warned against "repudiating [U.S.] obligations under the [Geneva] conventions." Yoo's arguments were not just legally flawed but very damaging to the interests of the United States. Colin Powell, the secretary of state, agreed.

The strongest endorsement of Yoo's approach came from Gonzales. The reliable yes-man had advised Bush since their days in the Texas governor's mansion. He always knew what the boss wanted to hear. In late January, the future attorney general sent a memo to the president that endorsed Yoo's arguments and added his own.

"As you have said," he wrote to Bush, "the war against terrorism is a new kind of war. The nature of the new war places a high premium on other factors, such as the ability to quickly obtain information from captured terrorists and their sponsors in order to avoid further atrocities against American civilians." The new peril "renders obsolete Geneva's strict limitations on questioning of enemy prisoners and renders quaint some of its provisions." Declaring that the Geneva Conventions did not apply, Gonzales added, would avoid the possibility of American officials being subject to prosecution for war crimes under United States or international law.

The president soon dismissed Powell's warning that a century of American commitment to the Geneva Conventions would be costly both at home and abroad—and could endanger our own troops.

DURING THE WINTER and spring of 2002, a crescendo of terror alerts from Washington began, continuing with a pattern of rising and falling alarms that followed a clear political pattern until the 2004 election. Looking back it was not difficult to divine the purpose of the color-coded alarm system created by former Pennsylvania governor Tom Ridge, the amiable but mediocre politician appointed by Bush to direct the Office of Homeland Security.

At the time, the White House hoped to prevent any independent investigation of its culpability in the catastrophe of 9/11. Manipulation of public fear bolstered the argument, articulated by Bush and Cheney, that such a probe would distract them from stopping future attacks. But distraction was plainly Ridge's purpose whenever he raised the alert level from yellow to orange. A clever blogger known only as Julius Civitatus created a graph that plotted government security alerts against news reports that embarrassed the White House. In early February 2002, for example, as headlines and airwaves buzzed over the scandalous collapse of the Enron Corporation, furious Democrats and Republicans on the Senate Commerce Committee voted to subpoena Kenneth Lay, the company's chairman. The president's feeble claim that he hardly knew Lay, one of his top fund-raisers and a longtime family friend, was not going over well. A week later, Ashcroft issued a statement urging "all Americans to be on the highest state of alert" after the FBI warned of a possible terrorist attack.

An unmistakable pattern of similar coincidences, often only a day apart, could eventually be traced all the way through the November 2004 election. Another such convenient incident took place in June 2002, after FBI agent Coleen Rowley told the Senate Judiciary Committee about her attempt to investigate suspicious behavior of Zacharias Moussaoui before 9/11. The "Little Shop of Horrors" at FBI headquarters in Washington had frustrated Rowley, and she told the committee on national television that she believed the attacks could have been prevented.

The next day, Ashcroft convened an extraordinary press conference in Moscow, where he was in the midst of an official trip, to announce a "significant step forward in the war on terrorism." Law enforcement officials had apprehended José Padilla, a.k.a. Abdullah al-Muhajir, "a known terrorist who was exploring a plan to build and explode a radiological dispersion device"—a dirty bomb—somewhere in the United States.

Although the national media cooperated magnificently with this publicity stunt, the dirty-bomb plot turned out, on closer examination, to be somewhat less terrifying than advertised.

Ashcroft hyped the arrest of the former Chicago gang member and hotel banquet waiter, and praised the FBI and the CIA for "capturing Abdullah al-Muhajir before he could act on his deadly plan," but it turned out that the petty criminal really had no plan, deadly or otherwise. It also turned out that Padilla had been arrested in Chicago nearly a month earlier.

Despite the suspicious timing and exaggerations, however, Ashcroft's announcement was not without significance. Down below his breathless account of the nonplot, there was important news. Rather than charge Padilla with a crime, the government had designated him instead an "enemy combatant." The FBI had turned him over to the Defense Department, which had promptly deposited him in a navy brig.

Having kept close watch on Padilla, the authorities inexplicably grabbed him as soon as he tried to enter the country. With proper surveillance of his movements and contacts, the FBI could have rolled up any al Qaeda confederates he contacted upon his return to the United States. He might even have committed an overt act that permitted his arrest on conspiracy charges. What suddenly mattered more was that the extraordinary measures initially used against immigrants—indefinite detention without charges or access to counsel—had been invoked to deprive a citizen of his freedom. However mad or bad Padilla was—and he was likely both—he was also undoubtedly an American.

So was Yaser Esam Hamdi. Captured by the Northern Alliance during fighting in Afghanistan, turned over to American forces, and shipped to Guantánamo, the young man was believed to be Saudi. But while he had been raised in Saudi Arabia, Hamdi told his captors that he had been born in Louisiana. When that fact was established several months later, the government transferred him from the Cuban detention camp to solitary confinement in a brig in Virginia—and declared him an enemy combatant stripped of all normal rights. His status was made public within weeks of the Padilla announcement, when the Department of Justice filed its response to a habeas corpus petition signed by Hamdi's father. In the view of the United States government, Hamdi's citizenship mattered not at all.

And for good measure, the grandstanding Ashcroft had, with scant regard for legal ethics, suggested publicly that Hamdi had been responsible for the murder of Johnny Michael Spann, a CIA agent killed in an uprising by prisoners at a camp in northern Afghanistan.

All in all, the government's conduct astonished U.S. District Judge Robert Doumar, who accepted the Hamdi petition. He noted that prosecutors "could not cite one case where a prisoner of any variety within the jurisdiction of a United States District Court, who was held incommunicado and indefinitely, and who had filed a petition for a writ of habeas corpus, was denied access to an attorney or the right to file such a petition."

The Padilla and Hamdi cases, despite their differences, each represented a historic moment, and for the same reason: The American government had asserted the authority to deprive its citizens of the most fundamental liberties, which were not only enshrined in the Bill of Rights but long predated the American Constitution in English common law. Those denominated enemy combatants could be seized anywhere, whether in a war zone abroad or in an American city, shoved into solitary confinement, deprived of counsel, and denied the right to a court hearing.

On behalf of Bush, Ashcroft was reclaiming the prerogatives of a king. In theory their claim was absolute; it acknowledged no limitation that might be imposed by Congress or the courts, or any obligation to seek their approval. This outrage was precisely what the president's critics had feared and predicted when he signed the order for military tribunals—only worse.

.   .   .

DURING THE MONTHS that followed the president's decision to override the Geneva Conventions, military and intelligence officers brought to bear a variety of "forward-leaning" interrogation methods, including the water-boarding torture that simulates drowning. FBI and CIA officials who oversaw these brutal practices were disturbed, and worried that they might someday be subject to criminal prosecution.

Once more the Pentagon turned to Yoo, who responded by drafting the infamous "torture memo" of August 1, 2002. Through the device of defining torture upward, he stretched the limits of the permissible to include vicious techniques of coercion. Interrogators could use death threats and mind-altering drugs. They could torment prisoners mentally, and they could inflict severe physical pain, so long as it did not reach the same level as "organ failure, impairment of bodily function, or even death." But Yoo went further, using familiar language. The president could order the use of torture in wartime—notwithstanding the array of American laws and international treaties having the force of law—because the Constitution vested sole authority in him as commander in chief.

The disastrous consequences of Yoo's advice have since been revealed in copious written evidence and horrifying videotaped and photographed details of atrocities in Bagram, Guantánamo, Abu Ghraib, and several undisclosed locations. In the course of covering up the responsibility of the Bush administration's highest officials, including Cheney and Rumsfeld, and denying that the United States had authorized or permitted torture, the White House publicly rescinded the torture memos. The underlying theory of a supremely powerful president remained in force.

"I'm pretty sure that's an argument no one has ever made before," Yoo boasted to the *Los Angeles Times* after he had returned to Berkeley's Boalt Hall to teach law. Yet he surely owed an intellectual debt to Laurence Silberman, the irascible, highly partisan jurist for whom both he and Viet Dinh had once clerked. The influence of Silberman, who sits as a senior judge on the U.S. Court of Appeals for the District of Columbia, remains important, and not only because he pioneered the arguments now advanced by his protégés.

Silberman's own career dates back to the Nixon administration, when he rose to the position of deputy attorney general under John Mitchell, who went to prison in the Watergate scandal. Since then, as he ascended to the federal bench and nurtured the young Federalist Society lawyers like Yoo and Dinh who arrived in his chambers as clerks, he has assiduously promoted the most imperial (and Nixonian) interpretation of presidential power.

Yoo's mentor had long ago marked out the extreme position on this issue. In 1978, when Congress passed the Foreign Intelligence Surveillance Act (FISA) that George W. Bush has admitted violating, Silberman testified against the legislation, saying that it would create an unconstitutional hindrance to presidential power. Both the executive and legislative branches rejected that opinion when Congress passed FISA and President Jimmy Carter signed it.

Silberman has since risen to one of the most powerful positions in the federal judiciary short of a seat on the Supreme Court. He has also earned a reputation as a remorseless, bullying partisan whose jurisprudence is measured to the convenience of his fellow Republicans, most notoriously during the Iran-Contra affair. Defenders of the Reagan administration argued then that the president could lawfully ignore the will of Congress by secretly arming the Contras in Nicaragua and trading arms for hostages with the totalitarian, terror-sponsoring regime in Iran.

As a judge on the Court of Appeals for the District of

Columbia, Silberman joined with another Reagan appointee to dismiss the felony conviction of chief conspirator Lt. Col. Oliver North won by special prosecutor Lawrence Walsh. A life-long Republican, Walsh later said he believed that Silberman's open displays of partisan bias at the appeals hearings might have reached the level of judicial misconduct. The Silberman decision helped the Reagan White House to escape accountability for its blatant violations of law.

Predictably, however, the judge's view of presidential power changed when he reviewed the prerogatives claimed by a Democratic president. During the Lewinsky investigation, he denounced the Clinton administration's argument that executive privilege should apply to Secret Service agents protecting the president. He publicly denounced Clinton's resistance to the independent counsel's overreaching as "a declaration of war on the United States" by the president. David Brock has said that (in Brock's former life as journalistic hit man) the judge, years earlier, privately (and unethically) urged him to publish the most salacious, sexually oriented material in the *American Spectator* in order to ruin Clinton.

Silberman has denied the charges. Under a separate appointment by the late Chief Justice William Rehnquist, Silberman hears appeals from the decisions of the Foreign Intelligence Surveillance Court established under FISA. It's not a taxing post, given the exceedingly rare occasions when the lower court rejects a government application for a surveillance warrant.

That Rehnquist would have placed Silberman in a position to oversee the FISA court seems typical of a certain Republican style of governance, which perversely vests responsibility for enforcing federal laws in officials who disdain their purpose. Ruling on a sealed case in 2002, Silberman exploited that position to deliver an opinion that undermined FISA and advanced the imperial executive.

Alluding to the power to collect foreign intelligence information without a warrant, he wrote: "We take for granted that the President does have that authority and, assuming that is so, FISA could not encroach on the President's constitutional power." Of course, FISA was passed precisely to monitor and limit the president's undeniable power to detect any threat to the United States. Silberman's obiter dictum was clearly intended to suggest that FISA itself is unconstitutional and pointless—because the president can wiretap, search, and seize evidence at will in the name of national security.

Yoo expanded Silberman's theories to lend an aura of legality to the Republican excesses. The roots of his argument can be found in the chambers of the Nixonian judge who taught him how to undermine the constitutional limitations on the president. As the legal scholars Gene Healy and Timothy Lynch noted in a report for the libertarian Cato Institute: "The pattern that emerges is one of a ceaseless push for power, unchecked by either the courts or Congress . . . [and] of disdain for constitutional limits."

WHEN JOHN YOO called his theory of presidential authority "an argument no one has ever made before," he revealed more than his own mild vanity. As a conservative lawyer and a committed leader of the Federalist Society, whose symbol is a silhouetted profile of James Madison, he was an avowed advocate of limited government and strict adherence to the original text of the Constitution. Yet with the public support of Ashcroft, Olson, Bork, and other Federalist leaders, Yoo had overthrown those principles to promote a radical conception of presidential power and a sharp departure from constitutional norms. It was one thing to argue, as some Federalists did, over whether the First Amendment should protect pornographers as well as political speakers. It was another thing altogether to strip away the protections of the Fourth, Fifth, and Sixth Amendments in secret.

As the legal scholar David Cole observed, Yoo realized that he must try to overcome this contradiction. If he could not, then the actions of the Republican regime would forfeit any constitutional legitimacy.

"What Yoo offers that is new," Cole explained in the *New York Review of Books*, "is an attempt to reconcile these modern-day conservative preferences with an influential conservative theory of constitutional interpretation: the 'originalist' approach, which claims that the Constitution must be interpreted according to the specific understandings held by the framers, the ratifiers, and the public when the Constitution and its amendments were drafted.

"The problem for originalists who believe in a strong executive and are cynical about international law is that the framers held precisely the opposite views — they were intensely wary of executive power, and as leaders of a new and vulnerable nation, they were eager to ensure that the mutual obligations they had negotiated with other countries would be honored and enforced." The founders had fought a bitter war and risked hanging to rid themselves of an oppressive sovereign. They would not have looked kindly on a president who claimed powers that even the king of England had long since relinquished. The original language of the constitution was plain enough. Everyone had the right to habeas corpus and due process of law. Every treaty ratified by the proper constitutional process was the law of the land.

It was easy to see why the neoconservatives and authoritarians in the White House and the Pentagon turned to Yoo for legal advice whenever they confronted a legal or constitutional obstacle. He had fashioned an argument that allowed them to do whatever they wanted, without acknowledging their own contempt for the rule of law.

It was hard not to wonder whether they had ever believed in those vaunted originalist principles—or whether their vehement argument had merely served as a partisan instrument of their own power.

AN AUTHORITARIAN LEADER requires obsequious advisers who know what the boss wants before he does, and are willing to make sure that whatever he wants is done. Their utter loyalty permits them to deny inconvenient truths and forget everything that might be inconvenient to remember. Alberto Gonzales established his credentials as that kind of aide years before the newly reelected Bush nominated him to replace Ashcroft as attorney general. After four years, the president and his inner circle had decided that Ashcroft should resign. His style grated, and he had shown a bad habit of seeking credit and upstaging the White House. That would never happen with "Al."

What saved Gonzales from being completely contemptible was his inspiring rise from working-class Latino poverty through law school, a big Texas law firm, and the governor's mansion on his way to the White House. The same personal characteristic that might deserve scorn had also enabled his climb to prominence: He is a company man who always and instinctively provides the answers that Bush wants to hear. Whether the subject was execution of a Texas felon or torture of foreign prisoners, he raised no discomforting issues and erased all embarrassing problems. Gonzales was the ultimate legal lackey.

That didn't mean he was stupid, however. When the Senate Judiciary Committee questioned him during nominating hearings, he knew that he should deplore the abuses at Abu Ghraib prison, denounce the use of torture, and promise to prosecute any officer guilty of that offense. He endorsed the Geneva Conventions, traditional civil liberties, civil rights, and even abortion rights as "the law of the land."

Yet by then it was far too late for Gonzales to erase his role in crafting the Bush administration policies that permitted and even encouraged the abuse of prisoners. He carefully distanced himself from Yoo's notorious torture memo of August 1, 2002, which had defined torture to mean only the most extreme pain comparable with "organ failure or death." That memorandum had served as the template for an official Pentagon document blurring the legal prohibitions against such practices.

When the senators asked repeatedly whether he had endorsed the torture memo, Gonzales insisted that as White House counsel he wasn't supposed to shape or even comment on legal advice from the Justice Department. His only purpose was to transmit the opinion, which he had requested, to the president. As he described his job, a secretary or messenger could have performed it. He also claimed rather implausibly not to recall whether he agreed with the views of Jay S. Bybee, at the time the assistant attorney general for the Office of Legal Counsel, whose name appeared on the Yoo torture memo. Gonzales duly noted that the memo had been withdrawn (after it was leaked to the press). Indeed, the Justice Department officially withdrew the torture memo just before the Gonzales hearings began, in an act traditionally known on Capitol Hill as a "confirmation conversion."

Gonzales's bland evasions conformed perfectly to his role as the yes-man of the torture scandal and all the secret constitutional perversions of the permanent war. As White House counsel, Gonzales convened meetings to deliberate on these issues, and according to the *Washington Post*, he purposely excluded lawyers from the State Department and the army who might dissent from radical decisions — as they eventually did with great vehemence. Again, Gonzales knew what his boss wanted, and he delivered. He also understood that the balance of power within the administration lay with Cheney and Rumsfeld, to whom the president had delegated so much authority.

The yes-man routine functions most smoothly when someone like Gonzales sweeps away awkward facts and dissenting opinions. At one point during his nomination hearings, Senator Feingold asked Gonzales about an infamous case concerning a Texas inmate whose court-appointed attorney had mostly slept during his trial. That dozing lawyer had been central to the convict's appeal, and remained highly pertinent up to the day he was executed. Yet somehow the governor's counsel had omitted any mention of that issue in his brief on the man's request for a stay of execution, which Governor Bush of course had rejected.

Gonzales said he couldn't recall the details of that case but the obvious truth was that the faithful servant knew his master's preferences. He was well aware that the boss wouldn't care and didn't want to know.

Despite voluminous accounts of torture and even homicide inflicted on prisoners in Guantánamo, Afghanistan, and Iraq, Gonzales suggested that the entire problem was no more widespread or serious than a few poorly supervised soldiers on the night shift at Abu Ghraib. He accepted no responsibility for what he had set in motion by undermining the application of the Geneva Conventions and the traditional military observance of international law.

And he misled the senators about the president's adherence to the law. Senator Feingold pointed out that, according to Yoo's theory in the torture memo, Bush had the constitutional power to authorize unlawful actions. "Does the president, in your opinion, have the authority acting as commander-in-chief to authorize warrantless searches of Americans' homes and wiretaps of their conversations in violation of the criminal and foreign intelligence statutes of this country?" the Wisconsin Democrat asked.

Gonzales parried at first, refusing to answer a "hypothetical" when he already knew that such blanket spying programs had been operating for years. Pressed by Feingold, he agreed that "the president is not above the law . . . it is not the policy of this President to authorize actions that would be in contravention of our criminal statutes." Finally, Feingold asked, "will you commit to notify Congress if the president makes this type of decision, and not wait two years until a memo is leaked about it?"

"I will advise the Congress as soon as I reasonably can, yes, sir," Gonzales replied.

He had said "yes, sir," knowing that this answer was false as soon as it left his lips. However well suited to an autocracy, the model of the loyal dissembler is not appropriate for the highest-ranking law enforcement officer in a democracy. But the Senate confirmed an attorney general who can be depended upon to say "yes, sir," no matter what laws, rights, treaties, and liberties the president decides to eviscerate before his term is done.

AMONG THE MOST durable stereotypes of American political culture is that military officers secretly yearn for authoritarian rule and harsh brutality, while civilian officials and white-collar intellectuals supposedly cherish our constitutional order. Those old clichés have been proven false in the scandal over the lawless misconduct symbolized by Abu Ghraib. Among the most reliable defenders of the Constitution are lifetime military officers, sometimes bolstered by John McCain, a very conservative Republican senator who happens to be a highly decorated veteran and former prisoner of war and torture victim. Officers from all the services pushed back against the neoconservative Pentagon officials, the Federalist Society lawyers, and the academic experts whose advice led to torture scandals and the abrogation of civil and human rights.

In an effort to restore the honor of the armed forces and prevent future abuses, McCain joined with senators John Warner of Virginia, also a navy veteran, and Lindsey Graham of South Carolina, a former officer in the Judge Advocate General Corps, to propose amendments to the Defense Authorization Act that would institute standards for the treatment of military detainees. Having loyally muted their criticism during the 2004 election, the three Republican senators sought a measure of reform the following year. The White House responded with a blatant threat, conveyed by Cheney: Rather than accept sane restraints on future abuse, the president would veto the annual defense bill.

The quiet but powerful dissent within the military came to light when Senator Graham released declassified memoranda written by top Judge Advocate General officers. Pried loose from the Pentagon, those memos show that in early 2003, ranking JAG officers from every service branch had tried to warn against interrogation methods that violated the human and legal rights of prisoners in U.S. military detention facilities. In essence, the JAG officers worried about the effect on the military of policies that encouraged torture and other abuses prohibited under U.S. and international law. Those policies endangered American troops, who could be prosecuted in U.S. or international courts—and undermined their own protection against enemy abuse. The JAG officers could barely conceal their astonishment that the Bush administration would consider discarding decades of training and tradition for the sake of dubiously effective interrogation methods.

"Treating detainees inconsistently with the [Geneva] Conventions arguably 'lowers the bar' for the treatment of U.S. POWs in future conflicts," wrote air force major general Jack Rives. "How will this affect their treatment when incarcerated abroad and our ability to call others to account for their treatment?" asked navy rear admiral Michael Lohr. The "implementation of questionable techniques will very likely establish a new baseline for acceptable practice in this area," wrote army general Michael Romig, "putting our service personnel at far greater risk and vitiating many of the POW/detainee safeguards the U.S. has worked hard to establish over the past five decades." Those concerns appear to have made little impression on Rumsfeld, Cheney, Bush, and their advisers.

Instead, they were more interested in ensuring their own impunity, while those of lower rank went to prison—yet another hallmark of a corrupt and authoritarian ruling clique. In 2005, one year after the press first exposed Abu Ghraib, the Pentagon announced that an internal investigation had exonerated four senior officers responsible for military prisons in Iraq, despite previous findings of their culpability.

The army's effort to limit prosecution to a group of enlisted personnel—and to discipline only a single officer, Brig. Gen. Janis Karpinski, who oversaw the Abu Ghraib guards—was thoroughly rebutted by independent monitors. A mountain of evidence showed that Rumsfeld, along with former CIA director George Tenet and the army's top commanders in Iraq and Guantánamo, had authorized the lawless policies permitting torture and abuse. They knew—and when the consequences became known, they failed to act.

But then, as Marine Corps general Kevin Sandkuhler noted dryly in his own dissenting memo, those zealous lawyers in the Justice Department and the White House "do not represent the services; thus, understandably, concern for service members is not reflected in their opinion." So much for the patriot baiting of Karl Rove.

The angry JAG officers were troubled by the implications for the military and the nation of the imperial arrogance exemplified by the Bush White House. What kind of country would the United States become if we allowed our military officers to behave like criminals? What kind of country would we become if we accepted the dangerous theory—promoted by the Pentagon civilians and the Justice Department—that in wartime a president can issue whatever orders he may choose, regardless of U.S. and international law?

Someday, when historians consider how this president and his associates sought to overturn American values, traditions, and statutes in pursuit of absolute power, they will praise the officers and politicians who resisted those illegitimate maneuvers.

The Senate ultimately passed the McCain amendment to the Defense Authorization bill by an overwhelming margin of 90 to 9, albeit with many restrictions and caveats that undermined its substance. Forced to swallow his bluff and sign the bill, Bush responded with yet another reiteration of his belief that as commander in chief, the Congress could not restrain him. He attached a signing statement noting that the bill did not actually bind him, should he determine that national security required him to defy it.

Presidents have issued occasional remarks upon signing new laws for centuries. But the use of the signing statement as an instrument of presidential power dates back to 1986, when Samuel Alito, a young conservative lawyer in the Justice Department's Office of Legal Counsel, wrote a memo urging the use of such statements to "increase the power of the executive to shape the law." Succeeding presidents used the statements to dispute the constitutionality of statutes passed by Congress which they nevertheless signed—but none with the same zeal as George W. Bush. In an editorial on Bush's use of the statements, the *New York Times* noted that no other president had used them "so clearly to make the president the interpreter of a law's intent, instead of Congress, and the arbiter of constitutionality, instead of the courts."

When he signed the act reauthorizing the Patriot Act in March 2006, Bush adopted the same arrogantly defiant stance. After months of debate marked by increasing skepticism among members of his own party, the Senate and the House finally passed a new version of the act, which otherwise would have expired. Seeking to prevent excessive use of the provisions that permit secret searches and wiretaps, it required the Justice Department to maintain records of how those powers are used—and to report that information regularly to Congress.

After Bush signed the bill with a flourish at a White House ceremony, he waited until reporters and guests had departed—and then his aides issued another signing statement. As the *Boston Globe* reported, that document quite clearly enumerated a number of circumstances that Bush felt would relieve him of any duty to obey the new law. His administration would not file the required reports if they might "impair foreign relations, national security, the deliberative process of the executive, or the performance of the executive's constitutional duties."

The wording of the signing statement exuded contempt for the Congress. "The executive branch shall construe the provisions . . . that call for furnishing information to entities outside the executive branch . . . in a manner consistent with the president's constitutional authority to supervise the unitary executive branch and to withhold information. . . ." To Bush the elected people's representatives were merely "entities outside the executive branch."

The deeper implications of the Patriot Act have become all too obvious since it was first approved so hastily by a panicked Congress. The Republican regime saw the act and all the accompanying secret orders as an opportunity to expand executive power indefinitely, rather than as an emergency measure. Those steps would prove to be merely the first in a continuous trampling of constitutional liberty. What was only hinted in October 2001—the exercise of unchecked and unbalanced presidential authority—has since been stated plainly. What was regarded then as an offensive tactic—the demonizing of dissent—has since been revealed as a strategy for permanent partisan domination. What were only theoretical abuses—the wholesale assault on traditional rights and liberties—have since become institutional policies.

THREE

STATE SECRETS
AND UNOFFICIAL
PROPAGANDA

What happened was the gradual habituation of the people, little by
little, to be governed by surprise, to receiving decisions deliberated
in secret; to believe that the situation was so complicated that the
government had to act on information which the people could not
understand, or so dangerous that, even if people could understand it,
it could not be released because of national security.

—MILTON SANFORD MAYER, *They Thought They Were Free:*
The Germans, 1933–35

It is an easy step from restraining the press to making it place the
worst actions of government in so favorable a light that we may
groan under tyranny and oppression without knowing from
whence it comes.

—"Cincinnatus," arguing for constitutional protection of freedom
of the press, November 2, 1787

OFFICIALDOM IN THE modern state frequently seeks to hide the truth, disseminate propaganda, and discourage the publication or broadcast of unfavorable news and commentary. But without free access to news, facts, statistics, opinions, policies, budgets, statutes, and directives—that is, to all the myriad and multiplying forms of available information—citizens cannot fully exercise their rights and responsibilities. To curtail that access is to cripple democracy, which is why the highest priority of authoritarian bureaucrats is the control of words, data, images, and ideas.

In America, where traditions of free expression and government accountability remain strong, such centralized power over the means of expression cannot easily be achieved—not even in wartime. Yet that difficulty hasn't discouraged the Republican regime from seeking unprecedented power over what we can see, hear, and read about our rulers and their policies.

Effective control requires the imposition of the greatest possible levels of secrecy, which protects the regime from accountability for its actions; the promotion of narratives, themes, and stereotypes that support the regime; and the intimidation or invalidation of any source of information that doesn't serve the regime. Few governments, in the era of the Internet, can achieve complete domination over the information that reaches their people. (And not even the most libertarian permit absolute freedom.) At one end of the spectrum is our own historically open society; at the other end are Fascist, Communist, and other dictatorships in which all news emanates from the state and nearly all of the news is lies.

Americans are still mercifully distant from that latter condition, but the erosion of freedom and accountability has advanced rapidly since 2001. Virtually from the moment that George W. Bush entered the White House, his administration departed from American traditions of liberty and displayed a disturbing tendency toward authoritarian excess—including a willingness to impose harsh, unwarranted restrictions on information, ignore customary freedoms, promote propaganda, and undermine constitutional rights.

The advent of the permanent global war on terror has provided the Republican regime with a durable rationale for secrecy, a compelling theme for propaganda, and an irresistible imperative for curbing and harassing the independent media.

These strategies reinforce each other: If government can conceal real information from the press and public, it can more easily replace that information with propaganda; if government can replace news with propaganda, it can more easily intimidate the independent media; if the independent media are intimidated, the government can insist on greater secrecy, and less questioning of its propaganda.

To enforce this new dispensation against the claims of democracy, the political regime need not rely solely on the power of the federal government, but can also depend on unofficial allies—including a formidable private-sector media apparatus that often behaves as its servant.

TWO WEEKS AFTER September 11, the president's press secretary hinted heavily at this urge to control, and demonstrated how the Bush administration (and its allies) would handle dissent in a tense national environment of fear and conformity. At the daily briefing in the White House on September 26, 2001, a right-wing press gadfly asked Ari Fleischer how Bush felt about a controversial comment by Bill Maher. The provocative television host had gotten himself in trouble by suggesting that suicide attackers, such as the terrorists who had flown planes into the World Trade Center and the Pentagon, were more courageous than pilots who fired missiles at distant targets.

"I'm aware of the press reports about what he said," replied Fleischer. "I have not seen the actual transcript of the show itself. But assuming the press reports are right, it's a terrible thing to say, and it is unfortunate." Having duly denounced Maher's politically incorrect remarks, he went a step further. Standing behind the White House podium, which bears the presidential seal, he said: "And that's why . . . they're reminders to all Americans that they need to watch what they say, watch what they do. This is not a time for remarks like that. There never is."

Despite nearly unanimous national support for the president in those weeks of peril, many Americans bristled at Fleischer's presumptuous warning. The White House responded to the flap with a curious maneuver (and a different kind of warning about its own conduct and motives). When the official transcript of the briefing came out, the words demanding that everyone "watch what they say" had disappeared. When a reporter for the *New York Times* noticed the omission, an assistant to Fleischer claimed it was "a transcription error."

That explanation might have sounded more plausible if the White House had not been caught dissembling at the same time—for propaganda purposes—about an issue of much greater consequence. For two weeks following the terror attack, White House officials, including Vice President Cheney, presidential adviser Rove, as well as Fleischer, repeatedly insisted that a "credible threat"—involving a "code-word confirmation"!—

had convinced the Secret Service that terrorists were trying to hit Air Force One and the White House.

This frightening claim was meant to deflect even a whisper of criticism of Bush's decision to fly around the country on September 11 rather than return immediately to Washington from Florida. Only when CBS News and the Associated Press shot down those false assertions did the White House spinners back off, claiming that the alleged targeting of Air Force One had all been a misunderstanding by staffers, with little elaboration.

In a constitutional democracy very few matters are more fundamental than the physical security of the head of state, particularly when the nation is under attack. To fabricate and promulgate a tale about the alleged terrorist targeting of the president and Air Force One represented a grave offense against government integrity.

Claiming publicly that terrorists had obtained secret White House codes not only intensified public fears, but must surely have mortified American allies engaged in sensitive discussions with the United States government. The White House never withdrew the fake story. Meanwhile, the use of blatantly false information—to aggrandize the president and advance the regime's political agenda—became the standard practice of the Bush administration.

Precisely two years after 9/11, the bogus threat against Air Force One reappeared in the script of *DC 9/11: Time of Crisis,* the docudrama that aired in September 2003 on the Showtime cable channel, just in time to establish the theme of the Bush-Cheney 2004 campaign. Replete with scenes and dialogue created to burnish the images of Bush, Rove, and other administration figures, the movie portrays the president as an action hero, albeit one who spent most of that fateful day jetting around the country with no evident purpose. At one point, the movie Bush (played by Timothy Bottoms), frustrated by military instructions not to return to Washington, roars: "If some tin-horn terrorist wants me, tell him to come on over and get me. I'll be home!"

As Tom Shales of the *Washington Post* complained in his review, *DC 9/11* is "primitive propaganda that portrays Bush as the noblest hero since Mighty Mouse." Its worshipful tone should hardly have surprised critics, given the movie's origins in corporatist collusion between the White House and the entertainment industry. In the months following September 11, media executives vowed to place Hollywood's creative skills at the disposal of the war on terror. Moguls Sumner Redstone of Viacom and Rupert Murdoch of News Corporation called a meeting in Beverly Hills to rally the entertainment industry against terrorism. This patriotic endeavor coincided happily with the commencement of an intense lobbying campaign by Redstone and Murdoch to deregulate the media, allowing their mammoth oligopolies to metastasize still further.

What began as a nonpartisan effort to improve America's image abroad quickly shrank down into one project, designed strictly for domestic consumption: a feature-length White House political advertisement. While some reviewers compared *DC 9/11* with *PT 109*, the 1963 movie depicting John F. Kennedy's World War II heroics, *Village Voice* critic J. Hoberman offered a more telling parallel. To him the cable docudrama recalled the Soviet cinema of the Stalin era, which regularly featured "their infallible leader . . . as an all-wise demiurge in suitably grandiose historical dramas."

Written and produced by Lionel Chetwynd, one of Hollywood's most outspoken Republicans and a recent appointee to the President's Council on the Arts and Humanities, the movie was based on lengthy interviews with top administration officials, including Bush himself. Before production began, Chetwynd submitted his script for vetting by Fred Barnes—the

Fox News Channel host, editor of the *Weekly Standard*, and later the author of a simpering Bush biography.

The release of this heavily fictionalized, quasi-official film portrait of the Bush administration "at war"—and of the president as he wished to be seen—contrasted with the regime's insistent, instinctual suppression of actual facts about what had happened on September 11, 2001.

During the year preceding the television premiere of *DC 9/11*, the real president and his staff had, as Senator John McCain put it, "slow-walked and stone-walled" the joint congressional committee's inquiry into the circumstances surrounding the terrorist attacks. After the committee issued its censored report in 2003, the White House refused to declassify critical sections that might prove politically embarrassing—most notably a twenty-eight-page examination of Saudi Arabia's possible complicity in the attacks. Throughout the congressional probe, the administration proved so uncooperative, and so determined to conceal the truth, that senators of both parties protested publicly.

As a reaction to the administration's secrecy, bipartisan support for an independent investigative commission mounted. But just as Bush and Cheney had sought to block the congressional investigation, they continued to resist every effort to investigate the true circumstances of the attacks. They opposed the establishment of an independent commission, withheld information sought by the commission, and refused to allow administration officials to testify in open hearings. They eventually abandoned much of their resistance in the face of public outrage, fed by the angry families of the 9/11 victims. Only an extraordinary combination of media attention, political organizing by the families, and persistent questioning by congressional leaders broke through the wall of silence erected by Bush and Cheney. That effort, by no means completely successful, took nearly two years.

While national attention was focused on the terrorist attacks, the administration's propaganda blitz, and the wars that followed, the Republican regime extended an extraordinarily broad blanket of secrecy over its own actions and the modern history of the presidency—rolling back forty years of progress toward open and accountable government. The result is a fundamental change in the relationship between citizens and government.

FOR CHENEY, THE engine of the Bush administration's continuous expansion of executive power, keeping secrets is more than just a paranoid obsession. He considers secrecy not merely the symbol but the shield and even the substance of authority. Denying access to information is an assertion of power over anyone seeking information and accountability, including the media, the Congress, and the public.

Concealing the furtive and the underhanded from public oversight has preoccupied the vice president and his circle since the Watergate scandal three decades ago. As young men he and Donald Rumsfeld served together in the Nixon administration and then in the White House under President Gerald Ford, where Rumsfeld became chief of staff and Cheney his deputy. Among the reforms that sprang forth from Congress in the wake of Watergate was legislation to amend and strengthen the Freedom of Information Act. The toothless law, signed several years earlier by President Lyndon B. Johnson, essentially provided no deadlines for compliance, no means for judicial enforcement, and no appeal from bogus classification of documents. An overwhelming bipartisan majority in Congress wanted to strengthen FOIA, both to empower citizens and to discourage Nixonian abuses.

Ford assumed the presidency in that atmosphere of democratic ferment. Bidding to restore confidence in government, he had made a clear promise upon taking the oath of office. "I believe that truth is the glue that holds government together, not only our government but civilization itself. . . . In all my public and private acts as your President, I expect to follow my instincts of openness and candor with full confidence that honesty is always the best policy in the end." But within weeks, Rumsfeld and Cheney were leading a campaign to convince Ford to veto the FOIA reforms as one of his first acts as president.

Endorsing their effort to kill the reforms was a bright young attorney named Antonin Scalia, who had been named by Nixon to direct the Justice Department's Office of Legal Counsel. Scalia did more than provide a legal opinion on the FOIA bill. He actually contacted CIA officials and urged them to lobby the president on the issue.

Although the advice of Rumsfeld, Cheney, and Scalia was wrong both politically and on the merits of the legislation, Ford heeded their warnings about the supposed danger posed by a real freedom of information act. Foreshadowing the conflicts to come, the unelected president denounced the FOIA bill as an unconstitutional incursion on the privileges of the executive branch. His strident veto message infuriated Congress, which swiftly humiliated him with an override passed by enormous margins in both houses.

THIRTY YEARS LATER, Cheney has contrived to win the argument that he and Rumsfeld lost back then. Exercising power in the intellectual vacuum of the Bush White House, he has elevated secrecy to the first principle of government. There seems to be literally nothing that Cheney will not try to hide. In the Office of the Vice President, he and his staff have turned concealment into a fetish, both absurd in its arrogance and sinister in its implications. When Washington journalist

Robert Dreyfuss asked for a list of the members of the vice president's staff, including their titles and responsibilities, the answer to his routine request was an imperial no. The vice president's staff is a state secret.

"We just don't give out that kind of information," said spokeswoman Jennifer Mayfield. Dreyfuss discovered that researchers for innocuous publications such as the quarterly *Federal Directory* have routinely received the same curt response. A senior editor at Carroll Publishing, the company that compiles and publishes the directory, told Dreyfuss that the vice president's minions don't even bother to return his phone calls. Taxpayers finance the salaries of these public servants, but that means nothing to Cheney, who believes he can simply withhold their names, titles, and job descriptions.

"I really think they think of [secrecy] in terms of good governance," explained James Carafano, a senior fellow at the Heritage Foundation. "It's a very corporate style of leadership." It is also a style of leadership most appropriate to a corporate state, where business executives and government officials can collude and pillage without concern for the troublesome checks and balances of a constitutional democracy.

Not long after Cheney and Bush entered the White House, the newly sworn vice president provoked the first and still most notorious confrontation over his need to conceal. Only days after the inauguration in January 2001, Bush signed an order establishing the National Energy Policy Development Group. Better known as the Energy Task Force, and chaired by Cheney himself, this outfit was expected to provide recommendations for sweeping energy legislation.

As environmental and consumer advocates anticipated, it soon became clear that the Energy Task Force would function as a White House subsidiary of the oil, coal, nuclear, and utility industries. Influence had been apportioned to them during the campaign with an accounting entry for each industry that reflected its financial contributions. The chief lobbyist for the electric utilities, a Yale classmate of Bush named Tom Kuhn, had organized the capital's lobbyists to raise millions of dollars for the Bush-Cheney campaign. In a memo to utility executives, Kuhn instructed them to inscribe a tracking code on each campaign check "to insure that our industry is credited." As he noted in a memo later obtained by *Newsweek* magazine, "a very important part of the [Bush-Cheney] campaign's outreach to the business community is the use of tracking numbers for contributions. . . . Don Evans [then the campaign treasurer and later appointed secretary of commerce] . . . stressed the importance of having our industry incorporate the 1178 tracking number in your fundraising efforts." (That's called efficiency in government.)

Neither the White House nor its generous allies wanted this highly systematized boodling to be exposed when the time came to write a national energy policy. To accommodate the energy industry's lobbyists and executives without exposing them, absolute discretion was essential. It would have been most instructive to correlate those carefully coded donations with the names of the lobbyists and executives consulted by Cheney while he dutifully prepared their legislative menu of tax breaks, subsidies, and environmental deregulation. Those tasty, high-priced delights eventually surfaced, predictably, as the president's national energy plan, but the process remained opaque. It is always easier to steal in the dark.

Under a law known as the Federal Advisory Committee Act, any committee that advises the government and includes members from the private sector must meet certain requirements— such as open meetings, publicly available records, and a reasonably balanced membership. Environmental leaders, consumer advocates, and civic groups voiced suspicions that the

Energy Task Force had been convened in blatant violation of that statute, as did Democratic members of Congress. The White House responded by insisting that the task force had no private sector members, and therefore did not fall under those FACA restrictions. But when challenged to prove that assertion, the vice president claimed that executive privilege allowed him to withhold the documents that would show who was on the task force and what it had done.

In essence, Bush and Cheney were inventing a new doctrine of secrecy, under which no law requiring transparency could be enforced against them.

The administration's defiance provoked lawsuits by the Sierra Club and by Judicial Watch, a conservative legal organization that had gained fame as a persistent nemesis of the Clinton White House. Eventually, at the urging of Democrats in Congress, the Government Accountability Office (GAO) also sued the Office of the Vice President, seeking to enforce its legal right to obtain information about the Energy Task Force.

The cases dragged through the courts for years. Defending Cheney against the claims of the public and Congress in both cases was Solicitor General Theodore Olson, the former long-time chairman of the Washington, D.C., chapter of the Federalist Society. Olson gained a degree of national notoriety after press reports revealed his covert assistance to the Arkansas Project, a $2.4 million smear campaign against the Clinton administration funded by Pittsburgh billionaire Richard Mellon Scaife. (His Senate confirmation in 2001 was jeopardized by his failure to testify forthrightly about that gamy episode.)

Because their complaints were so similar, the Sierra Club and Judicial Watch lawsuits were eventually merged into a single case. Olson answered their demand for transparency with a simple claim of executive privilege. The vice president, he argued, need not even respond to the requests for discovery by the plaintiffs. The paired plaintiffs achieved significant victories in the lower courts, forcing the Commerce Department to surrender memoranda and other documents prepared for Cheney's task force.

But Olson appealed to the Supreme Court and won, in a June 2004 decision tainted by a perception of bias on the part of Justice Scalia. The high court's most right-wing member heard and voted on his old friend Cheney's appeal, not long after the two men had returned from a duck-hunting trip together. Recalling their effort to cripple FOIA in the Ford administration, perhaps the vice president anticipated that Scalia would support him—and thus carefully refrained from "peppering" the justice with birdshot.

In the GAO lawsuit, Olson argued that the agency, which conducts studies and investigations for Congress, lacked standing to enforce any demand for information from the vice president. That case ended in a lower court with a decision delivered by Judge John Bates, a Bush appointee who had previously served as a prosecutor with Whitewater independent counsel Kenneth Starr. (Bush has appointed several former assistants to Starr, the would-be perpetrator of a partisan coup against Clinton, to top legal posts and federal judgeships.)

Bates ruled that the GAO, too, lacked standing to sue the executive on behalf of Congress, despite the existence of a 1980 law authorizing the agency to do so. His opinion effectively gutted the GAO's lawful ability to obtain information from the executive branch. Comptroller General David Walker, the Republican appointee who had bravely brought the lawsuit against the vice president, decided not to appeal to the Supreme Court and risk an even worse decision engineered by Scalia and company. And in what would become a habit of the Republican congressional leadership, they stood by idly while the White House curtailed their constitutional authority.

With a partisan judiciary and a supine Congress, Cheney won those initial struggles for unfettered executive power. While the cases were being litigated, the White House took still more aggressive steps to institute a regime of secrecy that denies scrutiny by Congress, the press, and the public. The "war on terror" provided an ideal excuse and a convenient distraction.

On October 12, 2001, a month and a day after the terrorist attacks, Attorney General Ashcroft issued a sweeping new directive to the heads of all federal departments and agencies. Where the Clinton administration had advanced government openness eight years earlier by instructing federal officials to comply with any FOIA request that would create no "foreseeable harm," Ashcroft's succinct three-page memorandum reversed that policy.

Rather than encouraging openness, the attorney general urged the agencies to "carefully consider . . . the institutional, commercial, and personal privacy interests that could be implicated by disclosure" and promised to defend any decision to withhold information so long as it had a "sound legal basis." His memo emphasized the importance of "safeguarding our national security, enhancing the effectiveness of our law enforcement agencies, [and] protecting sensitive business information," which might be compromised by overly liberal interpretations of FOIA.

Ashcroft's message was perfectly clear, notwithstanding a few boilerplate phrases about upholding FOIA and the citizenry's right to know. The presumption in favor of free access and open government was dead. The effect of his diktat fell immediately on the public interest groups seeking to probe the Energy Task Force, by encouraging agency officials to deny their FOIA requests on technical grounds.

The Ashcroft memo was followed five months later by yet another governmentwide directive, emanating this time from the office of White House chief of staff Andrew Card. The March

2002 Card memorandum expanded the drive for secrecy by ordering agency and department heads to start withholding a new category of information deemed "sensitive but not classified." What this meant was left largely undefined, except that it could exempt any document that "might be misused to harm the security of our nation or threaten public safety." Which, in the minds of federal bureaucrats, could of course mean anything at all.

Card also reminded the bureaucracy to zealously apply exemptions granted under the Freedom of Information Act to withhold "a wide range of information" about both government agencies and private corporations. The predictable result, according to California Representative Henry Waxman, was the misuse of these loopholes to "cover up potentially embarrassing facts, rather than to protect legitimate security interests." Waxman found that the State Department, the Department of Homeland Security, and the CIA had withheld such information from Congress as well as the public—notably including troublesome but unclassified documents about rising rates of global terrorism and false intelligence reporting on Iraq's nuclear weapons program.

Not only did the leaders of the Republican regime wish to conceal their own actions, but to determine what would be written about them and their forebears in the future. It is the same impulse that has been observed among authoritarian leaders throughout history. Falsifying history for political purposes is far easier when primary documents and accurate data are unavailable.

"The Bush Justice Department does not seem to view the Freedom of Information Act as a law, like any other law, that must be enforced to achieve the legislative goal of openness and accountability," concluded Jane Kirtley, formerly the executive director of the Reporters Committee for Freedom of the Press. "Instead it regards the exemptions [from FOIA] as loopholes to be interpreted as broadly as possible, in order to thwart the public's right to know what its government is up to."

ON NOVEMBER 1, 2001, just two weeks after the issuance of the Ashcroft memorandum on FOIA, the president signed Executive Order 13233—which, in the name of national security, essentially revoked the Presidential Records Act of 1978. That historic law, passed in response to the Watergate scandal and Nixon's subsequent attempt to treat White House documents as his private property, had granted scholars, journalists, and other citizens reasonable access to those materials within twelve years after a president departs office. For symbolic as well as substantive reasons, the act represented one of the most important reforms of the past thirty years.

Not coincidentally, the first set of presidential papers to be affected by the 1978 act were those of the Reagan administration, including the documents of a vice president named George Herbert Walker Bush, and others involving former Reagan officials who have since returned to positions in government. Indeed, several months before the president issued his executive order, the White House had been maneuvering quietly to withhold 68,000 pages of confidential communications between Reagan and his staff, which the National Archives and the Ronald Reagan Presidential Library had previously agreed to release.

Alberto Gonzales, who drafted the executive order as White House counsel, quickly assured reporters that his aim was not to cover up "embarrassing" documents. Ari Fleischer, the press secretary who announced it, told the press corps that the order merely created an "orderly process" so that "more information will be forthcoming." It will, said Gonzales, "help people to get information" and was designed to "implement" the Presidential Records Act.

Those soothing pronouncements, like so many others uttered by the president's obedient flunkies, were the precise opposite of the truth. In fact, according to Bruce Craig, director of the National Coordinating Committee for the Promotion of History, the obvious purpose of Bush's order was to undermine and virtually undo the act. His directive set up insurmountable bureaucratic obstacles and removed effective control of presidential papers from the National Archives. Under his rules, a former president or members of the president's family can veto any request. Anyone requesting certain kinds of sensitive papers must prove a "specific need" for them. Both the present and former president would have to agree before any such sensitive materials could be released. If either president said no, the only way to obtain the documents would be to go to court.

With those long steps backward, Bush restored to the president a specious property right in materials and documents that properly belong to the public. Treating the chief executive as a sovereign rather than a public servant, his executive order was an affront to American values. His attempt to close the vault on history had nothing to do with national security, and everything to do with covering up embarrassments past and future. His motives were exposed by his attempt to grandfather the Reagan era documents under his order. Why would Bush insist on that provision, if not to douse any new light that those papers might shed on the dubious role played by his father in the Iran-Contra affair?

At the same time that the Republican regime sought to block future access to information by historians, journalists, and ordinary citizens, officials of the Central Intelligence Agency and the National Archives were removing from the public domain tens of thousands of significant documents that had already been declassified over the preceding decades—by reclassifying them. This curious process—reversing President Clinton's groundbreaking 1995 executive order requiring the declassification of most federal documents after twenty-five years—had begun to-ward the end of his administration, but accelerated rapidly when Bush and Cheney entered the White House. What started as a reasonable effort by Congress and the Energy Department to pro-tect nuclear secrets became an excuse for the CIA, the Defense Department, and the Justice Department to place tens of thou-sands of documents beyond public reach. During the first two years, from 1999 to 2000, the CIA reclassified roughly 10,000 pages of government documents; but between 2001 and 2005, they had removed another 55,000 pages.

As *Slate* magazine's Fred Kaplan noted, the renewed effort to hide facts that had already been revealed was the reflexive reac-tion of a bureaucracy empowered by the Bush White House. "With very few exceptions," Kaplan reported, "we are not talking here about secrets that have anything to do with 'national secu-rity' as anyone might reasonably define the term. In many cases, we are talking about documents that were publicly released—and have since been widely disseminated—after careful review by high-ranking military officers and security personnel."

When the program began, a State Department advisory com-mittee complained to Secretary of State Madeleine Albright that such massive reclassification of historic documents threatened to turn the official record of American foreign policy into "an of-ficial lie." But in the following years it became more than merely another attempt to whitewash U.S. diplomacy and intelligence and rewrite history. It was, along with the full panoply of the Bush administration's information policy, nothing short of an authoritarian power play against an essential democratic ideal.

The irony of all these efforts to suppress information and sti-fle the public's right to know is that they may ultimately have had the opposite effect of what their authors supposedly in-tended. (Competence is not known to be among their virtues.) The Bush administration's own "secrecy czar," a sensible federal civil servant named J. William Leonard who heads the National Archives' Information Security Oversight Office, believes that the explosive growth of unjustified and sometimes unlawful secrecy is self-defeating. In a June 2004 speech on the subject, a worried Leonard cited the Pentagon's classification of photos and other evidence of detainee abuse at Abu Ghraib prison in Iraq.

"I am struck by a simple question when I see examples of classification such as we have recently seen reported in the media," said Leonard sardonically. "Specifically, exactly from whom are we keeping the information secret? In the case of detainee abuse, we are obviously not keeping it secret from the detainees." It was no accident, he observed, that the same government agencies guilty of perpetrating such lawless excesses were simultaneously experiencing "a virtual epidemic of leaks"—which is the inevitable result when individual officials have lost faith in the integrity of the security classification system. Such a loss of faith is the precursor of the cynicism that eventually infects undemocratic governments everywhere.

WELL BEFORE THE midpoint of George W. Bush's second presidential term, most Americans had reached two conclusions about the war in Iraq. They regarded the president's insistence on the invasion and occupation as a costly mistake, and they looked back on the case for war as a stunning deception. The sense that the nation had been misled and even duped was reflected not only in polling responses on the war, but at a deeper level in the public's changing perspective on the Republican government and the president himself. The people had lost confidence in their leaders because they no longer believed them to be honest and trustworthy. The personal approval ratings for Bush had plummeted along with his job approval ratings—and the numbers for Cheney were even worse.

Yet those popular suspicions about the nature of the regime's campaign for war were touchingly naïve. Very few people in America or around the world have even a rudimentary understanding of the scale, cost, and purpose of the propaganda machine created by their government to manipulate them. A very substantial part of that machine was built and financed by the Pentagon neoconservatives; that is where any serious examination of the machine's workings should begin. So it was fitting, if not predictable, that one of the American military's most respected strategists would conduct a thorough investigation of that mechanism and its meaning.

The officer who performed that important service was retired Air Force colonel Sam Gardiner, who independently issued a fifty-six-page paper in October 2003 titled "Truth from These Podia: Summary of a Study of Strategic Influence, Perception Management, Strategic Information Warfare and Strategic Psychological Operations in Gulf II." Gardiner, who has taught at the nation's war colleges and was consulted by the Bush administration in the months leading up to the war, felt deeply disturbed by the blatant deception injected into American politics by the White House and the Pentagon. He came to believe that the administration's conduct had been irresponsible and possibly illegal—and that these methods had profound implications for the future of American democracy.

Gardiner's study examines more than fifty separate stories planted by the Bush administration before, during, and after the war for propaganda purposes, in full knowledge that they were false. Those stories ranged from the faked exposé of Saddam Hussein's alleged effort to buy uranium yellowcake in Niger, to the mythical Iraqi drone aircraft that were supposedly poised to deliver chemical weapons into American cities, to the invented rescue saga of Private Jessica Lynch and the rumor that Iraq's missing weapons of mass destruction had been transported covertly to Syria.

To Gardiner, this massive exercise in "information warfare" represented a departure from military traditions because its deceptions were not aimed at the enemy, but at the entire world and especially at American public opinion. Under both the Bush administration and its partners in Tony Blair's British government, "information warfare, strategic influence, [and] strategic psychological operations pushed their way into the important process of informing the peoples of our two democracies." As he emphasized in the introduction to his study, this was neither an accident nor a mistake: "It was not bad intelligence. It was much more. It was an orchestrated effort. It began before the war, was a major effort during the war and continues as post-conflict distortions."

Gardiner was well aware of the frightening implication of his findings. "In the most basic sense," he wrote, "Washington and London did not trust the peoples of their democracies to come to right decisions. Truth became a casualty. When truth is a casualty, democracy receives collateral damage." And he warned that this was more than an academic study of a limited phenomenon. "There is more to come. As the United States struggles with a post-conflict Iraq, distortions continue. Probably of more concern, major players in the game are working on ways to do it 'better' in future conflicts."

According to the Orwellian reckoning implied by the title of *Nineteen Eighty-Four*, this scenario had arrived twenty years late. But Orwell might have recognized the nascent Ministry of Truth in the specialized bureaucracy that Donald Rumsfeld had named the Office of Strategic Influence. Created by Douglas Feith— the neoconservative ideologue who served as assistant secretary of defense and was responsible for much of the bogus intelligence that was used to justify the Iraq invasion—that office had been established in the months immediately following 9/11. With an outsized annual budget of $100 million and a tiny staff, the office employed psychological warfare officers and Middle East scholars—and outside experts from Science Applications International Corporation (SAIC), a huge research and engineering firm that purveys "information dominance."

The new OSI was exposed in the press a few months later, most likely via leaks from angry military officers in the Pentagon's public affairs division. The Office of Strategic Influence was shut down, in response to public outcry over a department so obviously set up to disinform and manipulate. (It was not for no reason that General Tommy Franks reportedly called Feith "the stupidest motherfucker who ever lived.") But Gardiner and other expert observers believed that the aims of "strategic influence" had predated Feith's ill-fated initiative, and outlived it, too.

Indeed, Rumsfeld indicated that the OSI continued in effect when questioned about its fate at a press conference months later. "If you want to savage this thing, fine: I'll give you the corpse," he barked at the assembled journalists, whom he obviously regarded as the enemy. "There's the name. You can have the name, but I'm gonna keep doing every single thing that needs to be done—and I have."

The communications apparatus at the disposal of the Republican regime went well beyond the Office of Strategic Information and for that matter the Pentagon. It included the White House Iraq Group, a top-level operation then commanded by Karl Rove and Lewis "Scooter" Libby, the vice president's chief of staff who in October 2005 was indicted in the Valerie Plame leak case. Its responsibilities included formulating the administration's daily message on Iraq, in coordination with the Office of Global Communications, the White House command center for counterterrorism messaging directed by Tucker Eskew, a longtime Republican political operative and public relations consultant.

To skeptics, these offices seemed to have been designed and staffed for purposes of domestic politics rather than international influence. Daniel Kuehl, a retired air force lieutenant colonel who directs a course program on information strategies at the National Defense University, told the *Columbia Journalism Review* in 2006 that his suspicions had been confirmed by the office's dismal performance in shaping world opinion.

"In my opinion, the global issue wasn't the reason why they were created," Kuehl explained. "They clearly had a completely domestic focus. They were part of the effort to re-elect the president. . . . I'm going to be real pejorative here: Their goal was psychological operations on the American voting public. That was part of the political arm doing that . . . [and] not long after the election, the Office of Global Communications no longer existed." Or it existed in name only, without a director or an updated Web site. In the meantime, Tucker Eskew had departed government to establish a private PR company in Washington — and to devote himself to the Bush-Cheney 2004 campaign.

WHATEVER THE CHANGING organizational charts of the Pentagon and the White House might show, Rumsfeld knew that he could "keep doing every single thing" that the Republican strategy of information warfare required. He could do it, moreover, in the style that he and his fellow conservatives liked best, because he had long since privatized much of the propaganda machine.

Major elements of the campaign identified by Sam Gardiner were contracted out, at a total cost of hundreds of millions of dollars, to a few public relations firms that specialize in "strategic information operations." The largest and most powerful of these organizations is the Rendon Group, headed by the veteran Washington PR executive John Rendon, who enjoys describing himself as an "information warrior." As the preeminent intelligence expert James Bamford reported in "The Man Who Sold the War," a path-breaking investigation published in November 2005 by *Rolling Stone* magazine, Rendon's company has participated in nearly every American conflict abroad during the past three decades.

With millions of dollars in contracts provided by the CIA and the Defense Department, the Rendon Group essentially created and operated the Iraqi National Congress, the exile group headed by Ahmed Chalabi, an American-educated banker and politician favored by neoconservatives as Saddam's successor. The INC served as the conduit for faked information on WMD, which was funneled in the form of "exclusive" scoops to prominent reporters—most famously Judith Miller of the *New York Times*. The INC convinced Miller to publish the unverified (and entirely false) testimony of supposed Iraqi defectors whose tales about dozens of weapons sites in, around, and under Baghdad then appeared on the front page of the *Times*. The impact of her articles during the two years leading up to the invasion of Iraq was enormous—and largely the product of a secret government propaganda operation.

Such operations persisted and expanded long after the president had declared "mission accomplished," and indeed long after Sam Gardiner completed his seminal study. The Rendon Group continues to serve as a prime Pentagon contractor for information warfare. In order to deter inquisitive journalists and members of Congress from asking too many questions about such contracts, they are always classified secret. But the facts about these dubious deals occasionally leak out—as in the case of the Lincoln Group, a very peculiar firm that has worked with Rendon and independently on the Iraq portfolio.

Initially operating under the name Iraqex, Ltd., the young principals of the Lincoln Group appeared out of nowhere in 2004 to provide basic PR services to the Coalition Provisional

Authority in Baghdad. The mysterious firm appeared to be run by a Marine Corps veteran named Page Craig and a New York–based, British-born businessman known as Christian Bailey (the son of a Polish family from Sussex, England, he had changed his surname at some point from Josefowicz). Both were in their early thirties, and while Bailey had been educated at Oxford, neither he nor Craig had any significant experience in media or public relations. What Bailey did possess were close connections with Bush fund-raisers in New York, where he had helped to run a club for wealthy young Republicans called Lead 21, which he described as "the big supporters, the big donors to the Republican party in five years' time."

While scouting for investment opportunities in post-Saddam Iraq, Bailey and Craig entered into a partnership with Rendon. That may have helped them convince the Pentagon to award their firm, renamed the Lincoln Group, a $5 million contract to "accurately inform the Iraqi people of the Coalition's goals and gain their support." Soon there were more contracts, which came with a new focus on "information warfare" and strategic psychological operations. In plain English, this turned out to mean planting fake stories in the burgeoning post-Saddam Iraqi press—and paying thousands of dollars to ensure that they would be published or broadcast.

Written by American soldiers assigned to an "information operations" group, and filled with fabricated quotations and invented facts praising the government or touting the courage of the new Iraqi armed forces, these articles would then be placed in Iraqi newspapers by local employees who served as bagmen. (The Lincoln Group paid up to $2,000 for the publication of each article, and placed fewer than ten articles a week; the firm charged the Pentagon $80,000 a week for its services.) None of these stories had any relationship to reality in Iraq. They were intended to be another form of war against the Iraqis. And of course they were an utter betrayal of the aspirations toward democracy and freedom officially encouraged by the United States.

But this wildly expensive fraud didn't work out very well for anyone except the profiteers. As an army public affairs officer later explained, "The problem was they couldn't do a third of what they said they were going to do. . . . They were sending guys over there that had absolutely no knowledge of Iraqis whatsoever. It was like the Young Republican fucking group—some guy who was working for the governor-elect in Michigan, a guy from the Beltway who was part of some Republicans for Democracy group—not a fucking clue. It was a scheme written up on a cocktail napkin in D.C. They were just completely inept." Despite their dismal track record, however—and the understandable reluctance of many military officers to work with them at all—the Lincoln Group continues to receive huge, lucrative contracts from the Pentagon. So does the Rendon Group. Strategic information operations, with their sinister blowback into American politics and media, will be the future template for the Republican regime's permanent war.

TO ANYONE PAYING careful attention to the American media during the Bush years, the stories of the Lincoln Group, the Rendon Group, and their pursuit of information warfare will seem ominously familiar. While the Republicans enjoy an enormous partisan advantage in the broad panoply of media organizations dedicated to its ideology, the White House and other federal agencies have nevertheless spent hundreds of millions of taxpayer dollars on domestic propaganda as well.

Actually, the correct number can be figured in billions. According to a study prepared at the behest of Democratic members of Congress, and released last year by the Government Accountability Office, the Bush administration spent $1.6 billion on public relations and media contracts between January 2003 and June 2005—but those were based on reports from only seven federal departments. By far the largest spender was the Defense Department, whose propaganda budget reached $1.1 billion. But the Department of Health and Human Services, the Department of Homeland Security, and the Treasury Department also spent hundreds of millions on public messaging. These amounts reflected a near doubling of PR budgets over comparable periods during the previous administration.

Government advertising and PR campaigns ranged from ordinary public service announcements to innocuously wasteful projects (the Air Force spent $35,000 on a "golf program" that included embroidered golf towels and souvenir golf tees) to blatantly political endeavors, such as promotion of Social Security privatization emanating from the Treasury, or the Healthy Marriage Initiative mounted by the Department of Health and Human Services.

Even more disturbing is the growing epidemic of video news releases produced by PR firms and aired on television stations as if they were news stories—when they are instead carefully designed propaganda pieces carrying disguised government (or corporate) messages. Whether sent by messenger or by the more sophisticated satellite feeds, these deceptive videos arrive in newsrooms around the country every day. The Bush administration has used VNRs, as they're called, to encourage support for the war in Iraq and to argue for the president's version of Medicare reform. The worst example of the latter involved a phony reporter named Karen Ryan, who appeared in a series of VNRs that closely resembled real news reports. Ryan was a flack paid to impersonate a reporter on TV.

Prodded by public interest groups, the Federal Communications Commission opened an investigation of whether TV stations were violating the terms of their licenses by broadcasting these video "stories" without disclosing their real origins. The likelihood is that many more are broadcast every day than the most diligent public-interest monitors can detect.

The Bush administration's propensity for concealed propaganda extended well beyond fake broadcast stories. Early in 2005, newspaper reports revealed what soon became known as the "payola pundit" scandal. Laundered through public relations companies, the Department of Education and the Department of Health and Human Services had awarded fat promotional contracts to three newspaper columnists—Armstrong Williams, Maggie Gallagher, and a relatively obscure writer named Mike McManus.

Columnist and broadcaster Williams, who was secretly paid more than $240,000 by the Department of Education to promote the No Child Left Behind program, suggested that he was innocent of serious wrongdoing because "it's something I believe in." (Evidently he believed that if he had disclosed his covert federal funding when he talked about that program, he would have had his journalistic ethics in order.) A paid publicity flack and shill for the Republicans, he, too, played a journalist on TV and radio and in newspapers. (Amazingly, he continues to enjoy a career in New York City as a talk radio broadcaster.)

As a ubiquitous presence on cable channels from CNN to Fox to CNBC, Williams flacked for Bush whenever he could get in front of a camera. (He could and did blather about anything, whether he knew what he was talking about or not.) Most of his commentary had nothing to do with education, but that doesn't mean the Republicans didn't get their money's worth. After funds started flowing from the U.S. Treasury to Williams's bank account, his column topics included the president's outstanding appointments of blacks to his cabinet, the flip-flopping perfidy of Democratic presidential nominee John Kerry (more than once),

Bush's superior morality, Bush's innovative domestic policies, and Bush's unwavering stance against terror.

Gallagher, a longtime syndicated columnist and GOP partisan, was paid about $41,500 by the Department of Health and Human Services in 2002 and 2003 to "promote marriage." She claimed to have forgotten about those contracts when she wrote about the Bush administration's marriage-promotion policy (which, of course, she believes in, too). But she really didn't think she had done anything wrong, either.

"Until today," she wrote in response to a *Washington Post* article on the scandal, "researchers and scholars have not generally been expected to disclose a government-funded research project when they later wrote about their field of expertise in the popular press or in scholarly journals. For these reasons, it simply never occurred to me there was a need to disclose this information."

Gallagher was less flamboyant than Williams (which probably had nothing to do with her much lower compensation) but no less ardent. He didn't have to write about education to polish up the president, and she didn't have to write about marriage to do likewise.

When her deal with HHS began, Gallagher testified at length in print to the greatness of the commander in chief. He is the nation's "Daddy," she gushed, and every bit as clever as those liberal elitists who used to look down on him. Her encomium concluded with praise for "Bush's genius"—and she wasn't kidding. She was still writing the same kind of pap years later, when she scolded the *New York Times* for doing actual journalism about the war on terror and criticizing the president.

It was astonishing that Williams and Gallagher—so typical of the right-wing punditocracy in professing to understand why democracy and freedom are superior to tyranny—did not comprehend why pundit payola is so repugnant in a free society. Scribblers subsidized by the state to glorify the Dear Leader tend to be found today in places like North Korea, Iran, and China. Yet that is precisely what Williams and Gallagher did; while quietly taking great wads of cash from the Bush administration, they promoted the president and his party, as well as his policies, and denigrated the opposition. Only in a degenerated media culture could they—and the government—get away with this outrage.

THE PETTY SCANDALS of payola punditry and fake TV reporters represented small yet visible missteps by a government determined to control public opinion with the public's money. The Republican regime conducted a far more significant assault on the Corporation for Public Broadcasting (CPB), openly seeking to impose ideological supervision over the nationwide public television network. Conservatives have warned Americans for years that the liberal commissars of political correctness would someday foist their opinions on the rest of us using our own tax dollars. In reality they became the commissars, with their own politically correct conservative orthodoxy and Republican party line.

Not long after Bush appointed Kenneth Tomlinson to head the CPB (2003), the new chairman began to extend partisan political control over the network with all the subtlety of an old-style Soviet hack. As a former *Reader's Digest* editor and Republican appointee, he knew what Rove had chosen him to do.

He quickly hired a Bush White House communications flack named Mary Catherine Andrews to set up a new "office of the ombudsman" to oversee the ideological content of public television and radio broadcasts. Prior to joining the CPB, Andrews had served as director of the White House Office of Global Communications. So eager was she to get to work in her new post that she began while still under the watchful eye of

Karl Rove, the president's chief political adviser and a longtime crony of Tomlinson.

According to the *New York Times*, Ms. Andrews "helped draft the office's guiding principles, set up a Web page and prepared a news release about the appointment of the [two] new ombudsmen," whom she apparently helped to select.

One of the ombudsmen was another former *Reader's Digest* editor known for his conservative Republicanism, while the other was a retired TV correspondent who had endorsed the GOP candidate for governor of Indiana and held a fellowship at the right-wing Hudson Institute. Thus did the Bush administration propose to ensure objective and balanced broadcasting.

Tomlinson secretly hired a consultant to inspect the content of *NOW with Bill Moyers*, the public TV program that most often irritated the Republican right. The consultant predictably tarred Moyers as anti-Bush, despite the many conservative guests on his program, from which he was ultimately evicted. The veteran journalist had been branded an enemy of the state.

It was in Tomlinson's engineering of top appointments, however, that his urge to mimic the authoritarian style approached parody. Having ousted the former CPB president, whose ideological leanings were deemed suspicious, he replaced her with yet another Republican placeholder, soon to be replaced by Patricia Harrison—a State Department official and former cochairwoman of the Republican National Committee.

Under the tutelage of Rove, the Republicans placed the Corporation for Public Broadcasting, with executive authority and $400 million in federal funding, under the control of a former party leader. Had Bill Clinton dared to choose a former Democratic Party chair to oversee public broadcasting, every right-thinking pundit and politician would have screamed for the immediate and total defunding of CPB and the appointment of a special prosecutor, while making angry comparisons with Soviet Russia.

What made this partisan purging all the more disturbing was the placid conservative conformity of public television even before the arrival of Tomlinson. Contrary to myths about liberal bias, conservative programming had been featured on PBS for nearly four decades, dating back to William F. Buckley Jr.'s inaugural broadcast of *Firing Line* in 1966.

The impressive roster of conservative and corporate-oriented programming aired on PBS airwaves over the years has included *The McLaughlin Group*, Peggy Noonan on *Values*, Ben Wattenberg's *Think Tank*, Adam Smith's *Money World*, *Wall Street Week*, *National Desk* featuring Laura Ingraham, Fred Barnes, and Larry Elder, and Tucker Carlson's *Unfiltered*. (The last was truly quality television, hosted by the same urbane wit who once quipped that "grouchy feminists with mustaches" run the Democratic Party.) PBS has broadcast many documentaries reflecting the perspectives of corporate sponsors concerning globalization, pollution, and other hot issues, yet has never agreed to a single program sponsored by a labor union.

Thanks to Tomlinson, PBS viewers were treated to a season of *The Wall Street Journal Editorial Report*, a program devoted to scintillating discussion among the ideologues responsible for that newspaper's ultraright editorial page. Taxpayers subsidized the production and distribution of this stupendously dull show, which was a failure on commercial cable. It is an arrangement the *Journal*'s editorialists would surely have denounced as scandalous, if only it hadn't benefited them. (The unofficial Republican regime network, Fox News Channel, has since picked up the *Journal* show, although there is no evidence that its audience has grown.)

Tomlinson moved on before he could be humiliated by an

inspector general's report on his activities, which found that he had violated the Public Broadcasting Act. Bush replaced him with Cheryl Halpern, a wealthy Republican donor with an equally strong ideological profile who has served on the CPB board and on the boards of the Voice of America and Radio Free Europe. As the board's vice chairman, Bush appointed Gay Hart Gaines, an interior decorator and big Republican donor with close ties to Newt Gingrich. Both Halpern and Gaines are intensely partisan and reliably conservative figures. In her Senate confirmation testimony, Halpern boasted that she had once had an objectionable journalist physically removed from the Voice of America premises. She eagerly agreed with Senator Trent Lott, the Confederate nostalgist from Mississippi, that Bill Moyers deserved to be purged from the airwaves.

Before Tomlinson left public broadcasting, at a time when he was said to be giving no media interviews, he showed up one evening on cable television to discuss his controversial tenure. The friendly interviewer was none other than Bill O'Reilly, demagogic host of *The O'Reilly Factor* on the Fox News Channel, where it is the network's top-rated program in prime time. At last Bush's broadcasting czar seemed to have found television that was more to his taste than the exquisitely balanced PBS. "We love your show," he told O'Reilly with a beaming smile.

NEVER IN THE history of American politics or American broadcasting has any media outlet been so closely identified with a president or a party as Fox News is with George W. Bush and the Republicans. Overseen by Fox News boss Roger Ailes, it is an inappropriate and journalistically illicit relationship that long ago crossed whatever normal boundary separates politicians and press organizations.

As a news executive whose smirking slogan is "fair and balanced," the belligerent Ailes has found the means to serve his politics and ideology far more effectively than he once did as a media consultant to Richard Nixon, Ronald Reagan, and George H. W. Bush. Although Ailes may coyly feign nonpartisan neutrality, his Washington bureau chief Brit Hume boasted after the 2002 Republican midterm sweep, only half-jokingly, that their network deserved the credit. "It was because of our coverage that it all happened," he told radio host Don Imus. "We've become so influential now that people watch us and they take their electoral cues from us. No one should doubt the influence of Fox News in these matters."

Even if the dour Hume was kidding back then, political scientists have more recently produced empirical data to substantiate his claim. Citing what they call "the Fox effect," professors Stefano Della Vigna of the University of California at Berkeley and Ethan Kaplan of the University of Stockholm found that the network convinced 3 to 8 percent of its non-Republican viewing audience to "shift its voting behavior toward the Republican Party." That was large enough, they estimated, to swing the extremely close 2000 election to Bush, especially in the state of Florida—where the Fox effect could have accounted for as many as 10,000 votes in a state Bush was judged to have won by less than 600. The two academics found similar trends in Senate races they studied and in the 2004 presidential race as well.

Fox News represents an innovation in the authoritarian mode: a fully dedicated mouthpiece for the state that is nevertheless unofficial and in the private sector. Such is the ingenuity of American capitalism, in the hands of naturalized citizen Rupert Murdoch, the News Corporation mogul who abandoned his Australian citizenship in order to qualify as an owner of American TV stations. Aside from profit, which only began to flow after almost eight years and roughly $800 million in estimated losses, the separation of ownership from the state affords much greater credibility to the propaganda message.

The Fox message is not subtle. Its typical content and delivery were demonstrated by anchor Neil Cavuto when he asked rhetorically, "Are Democratic leaders who criticize the war in Iraq actually aiding the terrorists?" The affirmative answer was to be provided by a Republican senator, without even a semblance of balance from the opposition party. Often the Fox anchors simply regurgitate Rove's spin, as the network's Washington bureau chief Jim Angle did when he accused Democrats of opposing surveillance of terrorists because they questioned the lawfulness of the Bush administration's actions. Occasionally the mask of objectivity slips even further—as it did when anchor David Asman referred to the Republicans as "we" during an interview with Senator Lott.

The difference between official and informal house organ can be difficult to discern. On Air Force One, the television sets in the presidential plane's press section were tuned exclusively to Fox News, until *Washington Post* reporter Jim VandeHei asked to change the channel to CNN.

"I was told, 'We don't watch CNN here, you can only watch Fox,'" VandeHei recalled. The White House press office denied that any such policy existed. Later United Press International reported a phenomenon noticed by many visitors to U.S. military bases: The television sets in recreation areas were also tuned to Fox News. And later still, The Smoking Gun Web site uncovered a White House document listing the travel requirements of Vice President Cheney. The television set in the vice president's hotel room must be tuned to Fox News at all times. Perhaps it was only a matter of time before the Bush White House hired a Fox News personality to serve directly as its press secretary.

When Tony Snow, the former Fox anchor (whose résumé

includes stints as a conservative newspaper columnist and speechwriter for the first President Bush) took over the press podium from the departing Scott McClellan, he soon demonstrated that he had not entirely left his old mentality behind. Answering a question about the president's position on immigration, the amiable Snow referred to a remark by Senator Chuck Hagel during a weekend television interview. "Well, as I pointed out— I mentioned this yesterday, and for—let me see if I can find my quote, because I pulled it out," he began. "Chuck Hagel, as you may recall, made a fair amount of news over the weekend when he first said that—let's see—'Well, I want to listen to the details and I want to listen to the President,' said Senator Hagel—he said this on 'This Week,' on a competing network."

In the White House, all other networks are competing networks. The special Fox connection is reminiscent of the collusion between a certain press lord and a fictional dictatorship, as imagined by Sinclair Lewis in *It Can't Happen Here*. After Buzz Windrip takes over as president, he seizes radio stations and newspapers to put them under military supervision. The only media property to be left untouched is the empire of William Randolph Hearst, who orders his editors to support Windrip with his trademark slanted coverage—and who develops a very special relationship with the fascist White House.

WITH BUSH EMBATTLED in his second term, as his approval ratings plummeted, the more independent elements of the mainstream media grew emboldened enough to dissent after four long years of acquiescence or worse. That shift prompted Fox News to act even more aggressively as the broadcast enforcer of patriotic orthodoxy—and to adopt a new role as a bullying adversary of free speech. When *New York Times* reporters began to file a series of reports on the Bush administration's surveillance programs, and their dubious legality, Fox News personalities and guests were quick to label the newspaper's reporters and editors guilty of treason. But Fox went still further.

After the *Times* reported on the Treasury Department's monitoring of international bank transfers for counterterror purposes, the talk of treason was amplified by outright calls for censorship. Morning host Brian Kilmeade, one of the anchors of *Fox & Friends*, urged the government to "put up the Office of Censorship," following reports in the *Los Angeles Times*, and the *Wall Street Journal* as well as the *New York Times* on the Treasury surveillance program (which was, incidentally, no news to al Qaeda, according to counterterror experts Richard Clarke and Roger Cressey). Echoing Kilmeade's demand for suppression of the offending newspaper was E. D. Hill, another *Fox & Friends* host, who wondered aloud whether the U.S. government should create an Office of Censorship.

The roots of that thuggish outburst, however, are not in the Fox newsroom, although such tropes will be repeated there and in other conservative outlets for so long as the White House seeks to intimidate journalists and critics. The intellectual foundation for the attack on First Amendment freedoms, in the context of the permanent war, must be traced as usual back to the neoconservatives. Specifically, it can be found in a seminal article in *Commentary*, the founding journal of the neoconservative movement.

In the magazine's March 2006 edition, senior editor Gabriel Schoenfeld suggested that the *New York Times*—and any other news organization that revealed secrets of the war on terror—could be prosecuted for violating the Espionage Act. Following a litany of complaints about the newspaper's editorial-page opposition to various policies of the Republican regime, including the Patriot Act and the invasion of Iraq, Schoenfeld proposes a response.

"The real question that an intrepid prosecutor in the Justice Department should be asking is whether, in the aftermath of September 11, we as a nation can afford to permit the reporters and editors of a great newspaper to become the unelected authority that determines for all of us what is a legitimate secret and what is not," he wrote. "Like the Constitution itself, the First Amendment's protections of freedom of the press are not a suicide pact. The laws governing what the *Times* has done are perfectly clear; will they be enforced?" Attorney General Gonzales hinted broadly that the White House might soon haul reporters and editors before a grand jury, even as the Justice Department sought to hunt down the government leakers.

If the *Times* management were convicted of any such crime, as many conservatives noted with bloodthirsty glee, the penalties could range from prison sentences to the death penalty — and might also include the government's confiscation of the most important American newspaper. Such a prosecution would represent the first instance in this nation's history of a news organization being punished for publishing state secrets. The overwhelming desire of the Republicans to achieve that awful distinction reveals the deeply authoritarian character of a party that prefers secrecy to openness, propaganda to facts, and obedience to freedom.

FOUR

THE CORPORATE
STATE OF GRACE

The clergy, by getting themselves established by law and in-grafted into the machine of government, have been a very formi-dable engine against the civil and religious rights of man.

— THOMAS JEFFERSON

When economic power became concentrated in a few hands, then political power flowed to those possessors and away from the citizens, ultimately resulting in an oligarchy or tyranny.

— JOHN ADAMS

As a result of the war, corporations have been enthroned and an era of corruption in high places will follow, and the money power of the country will endeavor to prolong its reign by working upon the prejudices of the people until all wealth is aggregated in a few hands and the Republic is destroyed.

— ABRAHAM LINCOLN, November 21, 1864

OF ALL THE potential perils to the new American republic, the prospect of concentrated power—especially economic or theocratic power—troubled the intellectual leaders of the Revolutionary generation. Familiar as the founders were with old Europe, where many of them had traveled or resided, they understood why the accumulation of inherited wealth led to inequities and imbalances that inevitably corrupted any system of government. They also understood how the establishment of a state-supported religious hierarchy had served for centuries to justify such venal tyrannies, while suppressing rational inquiry and political dissent.

After bloodily wrenching their nation away from the British monarchy, the Crown's mercantile monopolists, and the Anglican state church, the founders carefully crafted a Constitution that precluded such arrangements on these shores. While they hotly debated the future shape of the American economy, their views of the distinct roles of church and state were perfectly plain. Their opinion arose not from any prejudice against religious morality, whose benign influence they cherished, but from a determination to prevent theocratic oppression.

In the Constitution's Article VI, which requires every senator and member of Congress, and indeed every official elected or appointed to the federal and state governments, to swear an oath to uphold the Constitution, they added the clearest possible injunction against domination by any sect. All officials would swear allegiance to that sacred document, "but no religious Test shall ever be required as a Qualification to any Office or public Trust under the United States." In the First Amendment they drew the delineation between church and state even more sharply, forbidding any establishment of religion by the federal government. The existing state churches of the colonial era were disestablished and the oppressive clerical authorities peacefully overthrown.

If the imperial churches of the Old World bestowed divine approbation on tyrannical monarchs, then the vast agglomerations of aristocratic property and inherited gold provided their material foundation. The founders did not write into the Constitution the same kind of protections against economic oligarchy that they had erected against religious monopoly. But as revolutionaries devoted to self-government and individual freedom they could not help but suspect that concentrations of wealth would someday undermine those aspirations.

That was why Thomas Paine, the most radical thinker of that era, proposed a strict inheritance tax to fund a system of public pensions and social insurance; and why Benjamin Franklin, a rich businessman as well as a statesman and scientist, once suggested that "no man ought to own more property than needed for his livelihood; the rest, by right, belonged to the state." Adams and Jefferson, who became bitter electoral rivals, both supported the broadest distribution of land and progressive taxation to prevent economic despotism.

Historically, the state power wielded through wealth and faith in the European empires tended to be absolute, a characteristic in direct conflict with the philosophy of the founders, who preferred divided authority hedged by "checks and balances." They abhorred the autocracy of kings and emperors, popes and archbishops, all so inimical to self-government, freedom of thought, and equality under the law.

. . .

A CENTURY AND a half later, Sinclair Lewis envisioned a similar danger, which he illustrated in *It Can't Happen Here* by harnessing religious demagoguery to corporatist interests. His elected dictator Buzz Windrip reaches the White House in no small part thanks to the fervent endorsement of Bishop Prang, a fundamentalist radio preacher, whose millions of listeners fill the ranks of a militant group called the League of Forgotten Men. (That moniker anticipates the resentful style of the religious right, which constantly claims to be persecuted and marginalized despite its huge communications infrastructure, financial resources, and political influence.)

Just as the leaders of the modern religious right have suggested that George W. Bush's presidency is divinely ordained, Prang blesses the Windrip dictatorship as a "great Power which . . . Heaven had been pleased to send for the healing of distressed America." The bishop's right-wing populism, while promising social and economic relief to the forgotten Americans, serves as a deceptive scrim for policies that impoverish the middle class while enriching "a few hundred bankers and industrialists."

Lewis's 1935 depiction of a de facto alliance between right-wing religious demagogues and scheming industrial interests was inspired by real events during the early years of Franklin Delano Roosevelt's presidency. Among FDR's most potent adversaries was the popular radio priest Father Charles Coughlin, who began to denounce the president in 1934 as both a socialist and an instrument of Wall Street interests. Coughlin regarded himself as a voice for "social justice" and the forgotten working people, but in practice his fiery opposition to the New Deal bolstered Roosevelt's corporate enemies.

Those bitterest adversaries of the New Deal included not only the National Association of Manufacturers and the U.S. Chamber of Commerce, but the American Liberty League, a front for conservative Democrats and Republicans whose vehement denunciations of FDR often echoed Coughlin's broadcast sermons. League propaganda warned that the New Deal was steering the nation toward socialism and bankruptcy, and that passage of the Social Security Act foretold the end of democracy.

Although the Liberty League purported to be a group of concerned citizens, and eventually boasted more than 100,000 members, it was actually conceived and subsidized (with millions of dollars) by the DuPont interests, along with top executives of steel, oil, automobile, and banking corporations. Late in 1934, the League was implicated in a corporate-funded plot to overthrow Roosevelt and install a military dictatorship, sometimes known as the Business Plot or the White House Putsch. Marine Corps general Smedley Butler testified that representatives of the plotters had attempted to recruit him to lead a military coup; the existence of the plot was confirmed by a congressional investigation and widely reported in the press.

In the depths of the Depression, Sinclair Lewis was hardly the only American who feared that fascism might soon arrive on these shores, heralded not with swastikas but "wrapped in the flag and carrying a cross."

It is still hard to imagine a domestic conglomeration more toxic to liberty than an alliance of corporate potentates and theocratic preachers. Those are the forces that currently control the nation's dominant political party under the false flag of conservatism.

THE FORCES OF the corporate right are much more sophisticated and successful, if far less colorful, than their forebears in the Depression era. Over the past decade, the Republican ascendancy has been accompanied by the rise of a corporate political cadre tied more closely than ever to the White House and the congressional leadership. Long before anyone heard of the K Street Project—which was designed by former House majority leader Tom DeLay to regiment Washington's corporate lobbyists who congregate there within the Republican Party—the Bush-Cheney campaign of 2000 set up a computerized system that tracked every check routed from the various corporate lobbies and trade associations.

It is hardly a secret, of course, that the Bush administration and the Republican congressional leadership have been the most enthusiastic boosters of corporate power since the Gilded Age. Even though the mainstream media rarely discusses this fact with any degree of specificity or candor, the American public seems vaguely aware of the president's bias toward big business and big donors. What they probably don't understand is how profoundly and thoroughly the Republicans have integrated the corporate sector into the fabric of the state.

This oligarchic influence was reflected so broadly across the Bush administration and the Republican Congress that its achievements would be impossible to catalog in a single volume. Major construction and service corporations such as Halliburton and Bechtel have become the most publicized examples of corporate-statist arrangements in Washington, where multibillion-dollar boodling far exceeds the military-industrial complex that President Eisenhower warned about in his farewell address in 1961. Literally billions of dollars have been squandered and perhaps misappropriated by these companies in Iraq.

Equally disturbing if somewhat smaller in scale is the private mercenary business run by the Pentagon, which spends hundreds of millions of dollars annually on former Special Forces personnel to provide security in contracts from Baghdad to New Orleans. The biggest beneficiary of privatized security contracts is a North Carolina–based company known as Blackwater, whose president, Erik Prince, is a scion of the billionaire DeVos dynasty. Like the other members of the DeVos family, Prince is a devout fundamentalist Christian and a generous Republican donor. He has given more than $200,000 to party candidates and committees in recent years — and his company has received up to $320 million in government contracts, with little oversight or accountability.

In every realm of government, the White House imperative is to remove protections for consumers, workers, and soldiers; deregulate corporate management and subsidize corporate profits; privatize public services and government agencies; cut corporate and top-bracket taxes; and surrender public assets to private ownership.

Corporatist rule is exemplified by the writing of the Cheney energy legislation, drafted by the vice president and his aides during secret consultations with executives from Chevron, ExxonMobil, the Southern Company, General Electric, General Motors, the National Coal Council, the Edison Electric Institute, and representatives of dozens of other major energy interests. Lobbyists for some of those companies and organizations literally wrote provisions of the energy bill, while Joseph Kelliher, the Department of Energy's representative on the Cheney task force, served as a most humble messenger for his corporate patrons. According to the *Washington Monthly*, Kelliher wrote no white papers but "merely solicited suggestions from a cross-section of energy lobbyists and passed them on to the White House, where they were added to the task force's recommendations nearly verbatim." The White House then sent the legislation to the Republican leaders in the House of Representatives, who rammed it through with almost no changes.

The Energy Task Force was, however, only the most notorious

example of this pattern. Under Bush and Cheney, a corporatist partnership between government and industry has been grafted onto agencies that are supposed to protect the public interest.

Before the end of George W. Bush's first term, reporters for the *Denver Post* identified more than a hundred former lobbyists appointed to agencies that regulate industries they had recently served. To serve as the Food and Drug Administration's general counsel, for instance, Bush appointed Daniel E. Troy, formerly a leading attorney for major drug companies who had repeatedly sued the FDA on their behalf before being chosen to help run the regulatory agency. He soon offered to use the agency's resources to help his former clients fight lawsuits by injured patients.

According to the *Post* investigation, Troy's counterparts in other crucial agencies include "a former meat-industry lobbyist who helps decide how meat is labeled . . . [and] a former energy lobbyist who, while still accepting payments for bringing clients into his old lobbying firm, helps determine how much of the West those former clients can use for oil and gas drilling." The paper found twenty specific examples of the former lobbyists using their regulatory powers to benefit their former (and no doubt future) employers.

The platoon of lobbyists hired by Bush and Cheney was so stunning and their ethical misconduct so blatant—even when compared with the business-friendly administrations of Ronald Reagan and George H. W. Bush—that one of the White House's closest, gentlest friends protested. "In the Bush administration," said Senator Joe Lieberman, the Connecticut Democrat, "the foxes are guarding the foxes, and the middle-class hens are getting plucked."

Precisely the same process has taken place behind closed doors on Capitol Hill, where the largest industries have long since abandoned any pretense of contributing equally to both parties and have cemented their loyalty to the Republicans.

What once was a bipartisan split is now severely lopsided, with lobbyists and executives pouring hundreds of millions of dollars into the GOP treasuries. In return, of course, the Republican lawmakers permitted many of these loyal and generous representatives of industry to write the laws that affect their business. Tom DeLay cultivated a kitchen cabinet of important lobbyists who spearheaded Project Relief, which was DeLay's drive to sweep away regulations that protect workers, consumers, and the environment. Acting as agents of party, government, and corporation simultaneously, these lobbyists represent the cutting edge of the Republican corporate state.

THE PHENOMENAL REVIVAL of the religious right over the past two decades is a story whose outlines are by now as familiar to political observers as the rising influence of corporations and lobbyists. After the rapid climb of Christian conservatives during the Reagan years came the downfall of charlatans Jimmy Swaggart and Jim Bakker, the gradual eclipse of Moral Majority founder Jerry Falwell, and Pat Robertson's humbling experience as a Republican presidential candidate in the 1988 campaign—all indicating that the evangelical conservatives had lost heaven's mandate—or at least misplaced it.

Then, in 1989, Robertson decided to resurrect the remnants of his failed campaign to form the Christian Coalition, a grassroots, issue-oriented army of the faithful. By November 1991, with the help of a dynamic young party operative named Ralph Reed, the Christian Coalition was ready to launch its national operations at a secret meeting on the Virginia campus of Robertson's Christian Broadcasting Network, which attracted more than nine hundred activists.

With the national press formally barred from that founding meeting—and entirely ignorant anyway of the religious right's continuing existence—Reed and Robertson felt free to articulate their ambitious agenda. The shape of right-wing things to come in the years ahead could be discerned as Reed, Robertson, and their staff explained in meticulous detail how the Christian Coalition would take over the Republican Party precinct by precinct—and how that would eventually create the momentum to overthrow the Democratic congressional majority. But the most important long-term objective whispered at the coalition's founding meeting was to take control of the Republican National Committee. "How do you eat an elephant?" they joked. "One bite at a time."

Present at the creation of this putatively nonpartisan and tax-exempt "educational" organization were the era's reigning celebrities of the far right, from Gary Bauer and Phyllis Schlafly to Jesse Helms and Oliver North. But in hindsight the most significant guests at the conference were the top staffers from the National Republican Congressional Committee and the National Republican Senatorial Committee—the party entities whose biennial task is to win and maintain control of Capitol Hill. From their remarks it was clear that the Christian Coalition had already infiltrated the GOP's highest ranks. At the closing banquet Robertson declared his timetable explicitly.

"We want to see a working majority of the Republican Party in the hands of pro-family Christians by 1996 or sooner. Of course, we want to see the White House in pro-family Christian hands, at least by the year 2000 or sooner, if the Lord permits." With that last remark he seemed to suggest that the first President Bush—who was then in the White House and whom Robertson had denounced in one of his books as "unknowingly and unwittingly carrying out the mission . . . of a tightly knit cabal . . . under the domination of Lucifer"—did not qualify as a Christian (despite the president's professed Episcopalian faith).

Robertson ended his remarks with a prayer while his audience stood, closed their eyes, and held their hands over their heads.

"That we will see the standard of biblical values raised over this land," he intoned, "and that those who have mocked You and cursed You and cast out Your people is as evil will be put down, and that Your people will be lifted up. No, God, we pray that You will use us."

The real meaning of his prayer wasn't immediately apparent to the secular listener, but to the faithful his message was unmistakable. He was alluding to what evangelicals call "taking dominion"—that is, seeking to rule the nation according to their interpretation of biblical law, rather than the Constitution, in the name of Jesus Christ. He had once explained the concept on his television show, *The 700 Club*. "God's plan is for His people, ladies and gentlemen, to take dominion," he had said. "What is dominion? Well, dominion is Lordship. He wants His people to reign and rule with Him."

The following summer, in July 1992, Robertson and Reed showed up at the Republican National Convention in Houston with more than three hundred Christian Coalition delegates. This show of strength shocked the inattentive political press corps and the suddenly embattled moderates in the Republican Party, who realized that their old friend George Herbert Walker Bush had made a deal with these newly empowered extremists despite the insults directed at him by their leader. Bush lost that election, but two years later the Republicans won control of Congress for the first time since 1952, largely due to the extraordinary mobilization by the Christian Coalition of so-called pro-family voters.

Robertson's prediction that a politician who fulfilled his narrow definition of Christian would win the White House in 2000 also proved accurate—but by then, ironically, the Christian Coalition had plunged into a precipitous decline. Reed, whose scowling portrait had graced the cover of *Time* magazine as "the Right Hand of God," had resigned to enter the private sector as a well-paid consultant, Republican Party official, and potential candidate for elected office. Left in the hands of lesser figures, the coalition soon drew unwanted attention due to charges of corruption and abuse of its tax-exempt status, and ultimately forfeited its political predominance among conservative evangelicals. A host of other religious-right leaders and organizations, notably James Dobson and his huge Focus on the Family apparatus based in Colorado, seized positions of leadership.

The movement's underlying ideology remained essentially the same, however, and as their influence grew, its leaders articulated that worldview with increasing boldness. Where the smooth Reed had tried to present an unthreatening face to the nation, affirming the separation of church and state and declaring that Christians only wanted "a place at the table," his comrades began to speak more openly of America as a Christian nation over which they intended to assert control.

REPUBLICAN POLITICIANS AROUND the country responded to the renewed activism of the evangelical constituency with fervent declarations of their own faith in Jesus and their fealty to the Christian nation. Typical of these newly pious officials was Tom DeLay, the former exterminator from Sugar Land, Texas, whose devout pursuit of worldly pleasures had once earned him the nickname "Hot Tub Tom." Yet the political strategist who displayed the greatest appreciation for the full potential of the religious right was Karl Rove, whose friends knew him to be agnostic in matters of faith.

At best, Rove's attitude toward religion may well mirror the neoconservative or Straussian view, which upheld faith as a "noble illusion" vital to the preservation of order and morality in human society. At worst, he appears to be a cynic, determined to manipulate the faithful for his own political and ideological objectives. The border between those two perspectives can be easily blurred.

(David Kuo, former deputy director of the president's Office of Faith-Based and Community Initiatives, writes in *Tempting Faith* [2006] that Karl Rove referred to evangelicals as "the nuts.")

Whatever his inner motives, Rove had closely observed the impressive results of the Christian Coalition mobilization in 1994, when he ran George W. Bush's successful campaign for governor of Texas. Well before his client's landslide reelection four years later, he began to pull together elements of a presidential candidacy for 2000. At the top of Rove's priorities was to cement Bush's relationship with the religious right, whose power could not only propel a presidential candidate but also build permanent domination for the Republican Party.

Sometime in 1997, according to Rove biographers James Moore and Wayne Slater, the man whom Bush eventually nicknamed "boy genius" approached Ralph Reed, a longtime friend who had set up a company called Century Strategies to market his expertise and connections to corporate clients. He needed to prevent Reed from signing up prematurely with another aspiring presidential candidate such as John Ashcroft, but he also needed to act discreetly.

Ten years later, the deal that Rove offered Reed stands as a perfect metaphor for the Republican power nexus, despite the eventual fate of the central participants, who came to symbolize venality, dishonesty, and self-delusion.

Kenneth Lay, CEO of the Enron Corporation and a close Bush family friend, gave Reed a consulting contract worth nearly $400,000, ostensibly to help the energy firm campaign for electricity and gas deregulation using the muscle of the "faith community." Whether that made sense or not, the contract gave Reed the financial security to work quietly, "under the radar" as he liked to say, on the nascent Bush presidential campaign.

. . .

WHILE REED HELPED to corral evangelical voters in the primary states for Bush, Rove promoted his candidate to the decision makers of the Republican Party. He could count on evangelical leaders from the Texas governor's home state and certain longtime Bush family associates such as Jerry Falwell. Aside from Ashcroft, several other candidates were seeking the validation of the party's most powerful bloc: Gary Bauer, the former director of the Family Research Council; former U.N. ambassador and fervent fundamentalist Alan Keyes; and Pat Buchanan, the right-wing Catholic commentator who remained a favorite of the religious right.

The problem for all of those worthies was that the leaders of the religious right were quite serious about taking dominion— and that determination dictated pragmatic choices, not protest campaigns. George W. Bush was neither the brightest in the field, nor the most experienced, nor the most fluent in Scripture. He was the candidate likely to raise the most money, however. He was also a supple politician with a proven capacity to attract votes, and his name was an important asset. To close the deal, Bush needed the benediction of the Republican Party's most influential and secretive group of business, political, and religious figures.

In October 1999, the Texas governor went to San Antonio to speak before the members of the Council for National Policy. Like every meeting since the group's founding in 1981, Bush's appearance was closed to the public and the press.

Bush has never revealed what he told the assembled CNP members, but it isn't difficult to imagine what they wanted to hear. At the dawn of the Reagan era, Rev. Tim LaHaye, the evangelical leader and former John Birch Society activist who later wrote the bestselling *Left Behind* novels chronicling a fictional Armageddon, founded the CNP as an ultraconservative answer to the Council on Foreign Relations, which he regarded as the fount of the worldwide liberal conspiracy.

Named along with LaHaye in the original CNP incorporation papers were Howard Phillips, a former Nixon administration official and far-right activist, and Bob J. Perry, the multimillionaire Texas home builder who has funded dozens of conservative organizations. (In 2004, Perry would show up as one of the earliest and biggest donors to the Swift Boat Veterans for Truth, giving more than $4 million to smear Democratic presidential nominee John Kerry's military record.) Other wealthy supporters included brewing magnate Joseph Coors and Nelson Bunker Hunt, the billionaire oil and gas investor.

The CNP combined the two most important tendencies on the Republican right: the antigovernment movement that wanted to slash spending and taxes, privatize Social Security, abolish Medicare, shut down regulatory agencies, and unleash capitalism; and the religious right movement that intended to impose its authoritarian vision of Christianity on America.

Both Phillips and LaHaye had long been associated with dominionist ideas and organizations as well as political movements on the right-wing fringe. Working with them were Richard Viguerie, the direct mail entrepreneur and veteran of George Wallace's racist presidential campaigns, and Paul Weyrich, the founder of the Free Congress Foundation and éminence grise of the religious right in Washington.

Since its founding, the CNP has grown to include the most prominent figures on the right. Its four hundred members constitute an executive committee for their movement, including Robertson, Reed, Weyrich, Norquist, and Falwell, as well as Heritage Foundation president Edwin Feulner, Federalist Society president Donald Hodel, brewing heir and philanthropist Holland Coors, and hedge-fund financier Foster Friess. Speakers at its secret meetings in recent years have included Rove, DeLay, Cheney, Rumsfeld, Ashcroft, Gonzales, and Supreme Court justices Scalia and Thomas.

While the CNP enjoys tax-exempt status as an educational foundation, its directors cultivate an air of mystery. It publishes no magazine or journal that is available to the general public. Its Web site is difficult to access and contains little current information. Its three meetings each year are held at lavish hotels and resorts, with the highest possible security. Its members, who pay thousands in annual dues, and its invited guests are forbidden to discuss what happens at those meetings with the press or the public. But the speeches and discussions are usually taped for distribution to members only—and that led to an embarrassing episode for Bush.

Skipp Porteous, a civil liberties activist, spent years monitoring the CNP and occasionally succeeded in infiltrating a spy into its meetings. He had also learned how to order tapes of the CNP meetings from Skynet Media, the company that records them. But when he received the set of tapes from the October 1999 meeting, they didn't include the Bush speech.

Morton C. Blackwell, the veteran religious right activist and Virginia Republican leader who then served as the CNP executive director, later told reporters that while all the other speakers in San Antonio had agreed to include their remarks on the tapes, the Bush campaign had refused. "The Bush entourage said they preferred that the tape not go out, though I could not see any reason why they shouldn't," Mr. Blackwell said.

Ari Fleischer, then serving as the campaign press secretary, said, "When we go to meetings that are private, they remain private." He also claimed that "as far as we know, there is no tape." According to both Blackwell and Skynet, however, there was indeed a tape of Bush. In fact, the Skynet president told the *New York Times* that he had sent a copy to the Bush campaign. Fleischer and Blackwell dismissed the notion that Bush had said anything out of the ordinary to the CNP members, but adamantly refused to release a tape or transcript.

Observers of the Council for National Policy have speculated that Bush made promises about the kind of judges he would appoint and his administration's policies toward abortion, homosexual rights, school vouchers, tax cuts, and other issues of concern to the religious right. There can be little doubt that his appearance was successful. James Dobson, the Focus on the Family president whose broadcasts reach millions of Americans daily, bestowed his first presidential endorsement on Bush — and mobilized thousands of activists in the churches behind the Republican ticket.

Bush's relationship with the religious right leaders has only grown deeper since then, despite their occasional grumbling about the failure of the White House to advance their agenda by outlawing abortion or passing the Federal Marriage Amendment banning gay unions. His faith-based initiative has distributed hundreds of millions of dollars, preparing the way for an eventual transfer of government functions to the churches, in keeping with dominionist theology. Theocratic influences are reflected in Bush's public professions of faith, many of which signal his adherence to their ideology in ways that most Americans wouldn't recognize. Early in his presidency, for instance, Bush chose a hard-line dominionist preacher, Pastor Jack Hayford, to lead an inaugural prayer service at the Washington National Cathedral.

Perhaps the most disconcerting evidence of Bush's complete acceptance by the dominionist preachers came in the months that followed 9/11. That was when the White House, echoed by political and religious figures close to him, repeatedly suggested that God had ordained his ascension to the presidency, that he receives divine guidance, and that he is fulfilling the nation's destiny according to the will of the Almighty. Taken in context with his unconstitutional arrogation of plenary powers as commander in chief, these appeals to godly authority recall the theory of the divine right of kings. The theocratic notion of a sovereign accountable to no one but God was the fundamental idea rejected by the Revolutionary founders—and an idea exceptionally dangerous to constitutional order today.

IT IS SCARCELY a coincidence that the chief source of intellectual support for Bush's aggrandizement of presidential authority can be found in the Federalist Society—the influential legal association that brings together the most influential lawyers on the religious and corporate right. The Federalist Society's chairman is Donald Hodel, who also serves on the board of the Council for National Policy. Other religious right figures who hold important positions in the society include former solicitor general Robert Bork, Senator Orrin Hatch, and Edwin Meese III (all of whom are also CNP members). Included among the society's directors is C. Boyden Gray, former counsel to the first President Bush, heir to the R. J. Reynolds tobacco fortune, Washington corporate lawyer, and chairman of a lobbying group that promotes Social Security privatization (with corporate funding). Sitting on the society's Business Advisory Council are the chairman of Media General Cable, the president of United Missouri Bank, the chairman of Wachovia Corporation, the general counsel of the Investment Company Institute, and the chairman of Lowe's Companies. Those companies and many others finance the joint activities of corporate libertarians and religious rightists in advancing their interpretations of law and the Constitution.

The most fateful example of cooperation between the religious and corporate wings of the right arose in the struggle over Bush's Supreme Court nominations. After Justice Sandra Day O'Connor announced her retirement and Chief Justice William Rehnquist died after a long illness, the *Washington Post* foresaw a "potential clash with religious conservatives" looming for business lobbyists, who were seeking to persuade the president to appoint "an industry-friendly Supreme Court nominee." Worried over future court decisions on product liability, taxation, and other business issues, the lobbyists were determined to speak up rather than leave the field to the religious right. That decision "threatens to break apart the long-standing Bush coalition of corporate and social conservatives," the *Post* reported in May 2005.

The anticipated clash never came. Instead, following the aborted nomination of Harriet Miers, the corporate lobbies and religious rightists happily endorsed Samuel A. Alito Jr., a nominee whose pedigree and opinions promised exactly the results both sides wanted (and who clearly favored the most expansive view of presidential power as well). When Knight-Ridder Newspapers examined the judge's published opinions on the Third Circuit Court of Appeals, it found a clear pattern. Although he carefully avoided obvious appeals to ideology, Alito had "seldom sided with a criminal defendant, a foreign national facing deportation, an employee alleging discrimination or consumers suing big businesses." The Family Research Council declared itself very comfortable with Alito's highly conservative record, dating back to his service in the Reagan Justice Department, where he urged the attorney general to challenge the *Roe v. Wade* decision upholding abortion rights.

So well synchronized were the business lobbyists and the religious rightists in support of Alito that the Chamber of Commerce, the National Association of Manufacturers, and other corporate sponsors produced and broadcast a radio advertising campaign focused on issues that had nothing to do with free enterprise, their raison d'être. The wording of the ads was aggressive: "They [meaning liberals] want to take God out of the Pledge of Allegiance and are fighting to redefine traditional marriage. They support partial birth abortion, sanction the burning of the American flag, and even oppose pornography filters on public library computers." During the holiday recess, the corporate group picked up the "war on Christmas" theme popularized on Fox News and in other right-wing media outlets in their second ad promoting Alito:

> It's the season when Americans celebrate our traditions of faith . . . and once again religious freedom is under assault.
>
> Why? Because liberal groups like People for the American Way and the ACLU have opposed public Christmas and Chanukah displays and even fought to keep Christmas carols out of school. . . .
>
> Now, these liberal groups are attacking Judge Alito because he won't support their agenda. . . . That's why the liberals are desperately trying to stop Judge Alito's confirmation to the Supreme Court, and it's exactly why we need him there. . . .

Of course those religious issues had nothing to do with why the business groups wanted Alito on the Supreme Court. The ad was divisive, and inaccurate, but the ugly words served their purpose. By pandering to their faith-based allies, the business groups got their business-friendly justice.

CORPORATE MONEY AND church muscle put Bush in office—and kept him there—but not before Rove and Reed used the nasty Nixonian tactics they had absorbed as young Republicans to crush John McCain, his chief competitor, in the crucial South Carolina primary in February 2000. Although Rove and Reed left no visible fingerprints in those defamatory assaults on McCain and his family, the Bush campaign has been suspected ever since of responsibility for the anonymous leaflets and telephone push polls that asked "Would you be more likely or less likely to vote for John McCain for president if you knew he had fathered an illegitimate black child?," smeared his wife, Cindy, as a drug addict, and insinuated that the senator had been driven to insanity and even treason during his wartime imprisonment by his North Vietnamese captors.

The whisperers slimed McCain after his nineteen-point triumph in the New Hampshire primary and lined up Christian voters behind Bush. For years the enmity between McCain and the conservative operatives festered, even after he humbled himself with his opportunistic fawning over the president four years later. As for DeLay—who personifies the capital's bagman politics and did his best to frustrate the passage of the McCain-Feingold campaign reform act—he and the Arizonan have made no secret of their mutual disdain.

McCain had his revenge, however, when he used his position as chair of the Senate Indian Affairs Committee to open an investigation of superlobbyist Jack Abramoff in early 2004. He may not have been certain that a probe of the huge payments by Indian tribes with gaming interests to Abramoff and his sidekick Michael Scanlon would eventually embroil Reed and DeLay. But the *Washington Post's* first investigative article about the tribal gaming scandal mentioned Abramoff's long-standing ties with DeLay and Reed, and noted that some of the tens of millions bilked from the tribes had gone into the coffers of organizations associated with Grover Norquist, the Republican antitax activist and close associate of Rove.

An important side effect of the Abramoff scandal, as it engulfed DeLay, Norquist, and many other politicians and staffers, was to expose the stunning moral emptiness of the religious right's free-market ideology. The investigation revealed a dark portrait of Washington's conservative elite, whose behavior naturally repelled every American honestly concerned about moral values.

As Republicans liked to say during the Clinton years, the Abramoff scandal was a question of character. The best way to understand the culture of the religious right in Washington is to compare the morality of the business practices indulged by DeLay's friends with the family values rhetoric that kept them and their patrons in power.

Top dog in this predatory pack was Jack Abramoff, a lobbyist extraordinaire and former College Republican leader whose status as DeLay's close friend, fund-raiser, and golfing buddy brought him wealth and power. Known to his peers as "Casino Jack," Abramoff's operation and his associates conned several Indian tribes out of as much as $80 million. According to reports in the *National Journal* and other news sources, the Republican lobbyists played the tribes against each other as they competed for gambling permits and market share.

Among the consultants recruited by Mr. Abramoff to operate the Indian casino scheme was Ralph Reed, the evangelical Christian activist who founded the Christian Coalition with Pat Robertson. For a sweet fee of $4 million, Reed engineered "grassroots antigambling" groups that Abramoff then deployed to stifle the tribal competitors of his clients.

For a skillful hypocrite like Reed, it was simple enough to "get our pastors riled up" against yet another sinful establishment—as he boasted in an e-mail to Abramoff—because they understood gambling's destructive effects on families. At one point, he even persuaded Focus on the Family's James Dobson, probably the most powerful evangelical leader in the country, to organize opposition to a proposed casino in Texas.

Like Dobson, who often warns against the evils of gambling in his broadcast diatribes, Reed claims he didn't really know what Abramoff was up to. (Almost nobody believed him and in July 2006 he was trounced in a Republican primary for lieutenant governor of Georgia.) Yet the moralistic Dobson never spoke out against the crooked matrix that misled him so badly.

Still uglier than the Indian gaming affair—and more directly implicating DeLay—was the story of Abramoff's clientele in the Northern Marianas Islands in the Philippine Sea. The Pacific commonwealth is a haven for garment sweatshops that evade U.S. labor and immigration laws while legally labeling their products "Made in the U.S.A."—technically accurate because it is a commonwealth in political union with the United States. Nearly every big name in the American garment trade has dealt with factories there.

During the Clinton administration, the gross abuse of the laborers in the islands—mostly young women imported from China and Thailand—drew unwanted attention from the federal government. When Clinton administration officials proposed to crack down on the Marianas sweatshops and labor contractors, the commonwealth's ruling elite hired Abramoff to protect them. He sponsored dozens of luxury junkets to the islands for Republican politicians and commentators, spread around plenty of campaign money, and soon had DeLay pledging to defend the Marianas factories from U.S. labor standards.

The conditions endured by the women workers in the islands ought to have outraged any authentic Christian. Swindled, starved, and overworked, many of them were ultimately forced into prostitution—and when they got pregnant, they were forced to undergo abortions. Young women who arrived expecting to work in restaurants found themselves suddenly hustled into topless bars, where they were coerced into drinking and having sex with customers.

Promoted by DeLay and Abramoff as a libertarian utopia, the islands were actually a sinkhole of indentured slavery and sex tourism. Enchanted by all the easy money and free vacations, however, those Washington worthies and their friends disregarded the suffering. With sweatshops, whorehouses, and casinos providing the commercial underpinnings of some of its clients, the Abramoff operation was reminiscent of the old Cosa Nostra. Yet such unsavory parallels don't disturb the right-wing establishment.

When DeLay's sleazy methods caught up with him in September 2005, with an indictment by Texas prosecutor Ronnie Earle for illegal corporate fund-raising and money laundering, the leaders of the most important organizations on the right quickly declared their continuing loyalty to him. They were not troubled to learn that the prosecutor had charged him and two of his aides with allegedly funneling money from credit-card companies and nursing-home lobbyists to Texas legislators in order that they would gerrymander the state's congressional districts to favor Republicans. Rallying behind DeLay were the Family Research Council, the Heritage Foundation, the Free Congress Foundation, the American Conservative Union, and the rest of the movement, with everyone fervently declaring, amid displays of piety and indignation, that his defense would be their next great crusade.

Not many politicians have been as bold as DeLay in publicly claiming the mandate of God. His justification for pushing the impeachment of Bill Clinton, whom he accused of having the "wrong worldview," was particularly telling. While he cavorted on Scottish golf courses with Abramoff and gorged himself on Malaysian banquets, he was also assuring the faithful back home that the Almighty had chosen him for leadership and was teaching him how to do his job.

At one of many fundamentalist meetings he addressed during his legal tribulations, DeLay explained: "He [God] has been walking me through an incredible journey, and it all comes down to worldview. He is using me, all the time, everywhere, to stand up for the biblical worldview in everything that I do and

everywhere I am. He is training me, He is working with me."
Well, perhaps not everywhere and certainly not everything.
What did God tell DeLay about those lavish trips and dinners
and donations, and about the lobbying money allegedly funneled to his wife?

The actual Bible that he professes to believe is the literal
word of the Lord, is quite clear. Consider Job 36:18, which
specifically warns: "Be careful that no one entices you by riches;
do not let a large bribe turn you aside."

After winning the Republican primary with an unimpressive
margin, despite spending vast sums, DeLay resigned his congressional seat in the spring of 2006 with all the dignity, discretion, and probity that have marked his decades in politics. The
former majority leader stood before the House to deliver a
farewell speech blaming others for his problems, singling out
"liberal Democrats" and the "liberal media." He blathered on at
length about morality. He talked about "the enduring strength
of our principles and our ideas," and confided that he'd decided
to quit only after constant prayer.

The fact that his former chief of staff, Tony Rudy, had pleaded
guilty to federal bribery charges was merely a coincidence—as
was the fact that Abramoff, his close friend, political ally, and financial benefactor, had pleaded guilty three months earlier,
along with his former press secretary Michael Scanlon. Still under investigation was DeLay's former deputy of chief staff, Edwin
Buckham, an ordained minister and lobbyist who had also served
as his spiritual adviser.

In an interview with *Time* magazine on the eve of his resignation, DeLay boasted about the virtual monopoly of jobs and
contributions that his party enjoys on K Street, where lobbyists
routinely purchased access to the Capitol by following his dic-
tates. "Nothing illegal about that at all," he argued, claiming

to have achieved "total domination" of the lobbying industry, "legally and ethically."

DeLay was not alone in his responsibility for the congressional culture of criminality that has flourished over the past decade. He had many enablers, from the Heritage Foundation to the Family Research Council. Long after the character of his leadership became clear, Washington's conservative leadership paid tribute to him and pledged their unconditional support. Unanimously, they pretended to be blind to the spreading stain of corruption because he promoted their worldview. DeLay is gone—at least from the House of Representatives—but the money culture that created him and the corporatist "Christian" ideology that he embodied continue to drive the leadership of the Republican Party.

BETWEEN CORPORATIONS AND churches, the two major components of the modern GOP machine, there is an informal but clear division of functions. The corporate sector (and especially corporate lobbyists) provide the hundreds of millions of dollars needed to fuel and lubricate the party, while the religious right (and a few other related constituencies, such as gun owners) motivates and mobilizes the millions of volunteers and voters needed to win elections. The U.S. Chamber of Commerce, the National Association of Manufacturers, and the rest of Washington's vast network of trade associations and lobbying outfits funnel their money to Republican candidates, taking direction from the party leaders and mostly shunning Democrats. The Family Research Council, Traditional Values Coalition, American Family Association, Focus on the Family, the enormous religious broadcasting apparatus, and state and local ministries and megachurches send their devout followers into Republican campaigns while demonizing the Democrats.

On the surface, this confluence of corporate and religious influences may appear contradictory and fragile. The worldly, sophisticated, and well-educated executives of the American corporate class hardly seem, at first glance, like natural allies of the bigoted, superstitious, and parochial panjandrums of the religious right. Science and technology, not faith, provide the material basis for industrial production, and broad marketing appeal rather than narrow religious constraints ensure corporate profits. The creative destruction of modern capitalism disrupts traditions and disregards family values.

But while tensions surely exist between the religious right and big business, particularly in the entertainment and media industries, there is ample space for agreement on public policy. Many of the religious right's top leaders are very wealthy men, and their personal interests often coincide neatly with those of their corporate counterparts.

Maintaining this partisan alliance demands a high tolerance for hypocrisy on both sides. For the corporate libertarians, this means ignoring the religious right's efforts to break down the wall between church and state, to restrict reproductive freedom, to demonize and victimize homosexuals, and to denigrate science while promoting creationism and other crackpot theories. They turn their heads when the congressional leaders and the president of the United States pass a special, unconstitutional statute mandating life support for the vegetative Terry Schiavo—and Senate majority leader Bill Frist, a former heart and lung surgeon who prefers to be called Dr. Frist, claims with a straight face that he can diagnose her from a videotape. George Herbert Walker Bush was a perfect example of this kind of compromise—a former supporter of Planned Parenthood in

Houston whose political ambitions required that he abandon his scientific convictions.

For the religious rightists, the moral compromise with their corporate allies means looking away from the promotion of sinful behavior such as smoking, drinking, gambling, and salacious entertainment. Jerry Falwell and Pat Robertson may not like News Corporation's racy television programming on Fox, but they never, ever criticize their political ally Rupert Murdoch, the News Corporation chairman.

Whatever their differences, however, the religious right and the corporate right have much more in common. They hate the public sector, regulation, and government spending, except when they can get a grip on the federal teat through faith-based programs, privatization, and other contracts. They hate social insurance, welfare, and health programs, including Social Security, which the Birchers among them have wanted to abolish for sixty years. Rod Parsley, the Columbus, Ohio, megachurch pastor who is a rising star among right-wing evangelicals, parrots the free-market fundamentalism that serves as economic gospel. "I'm convinced the best thing government can do to help the poor is to get out of the way," Parsley told the *American Prospect* magazine. "If government reduced taxes, removed industrial restraints, eliminated wage controls, and abolished subsidies, tariff[s], and other constraints on free enterprise, the poor would be helped in a way that welfare, Social Security, and unemployment insurance could never match."

THE CHAMBER OF Commerce types and the Baptist preachers both hate unions with a special passion. Corporate leaders naturally regard unions as an impediment to high profits in the private sector and a drain on tax revenues in the public sector—and in any case they have learned that they need no longer cooperate with them even in a limited way. Organized labor, already severely diminished in previous decades, has come under unrelenting attack by Bush and Congress, who have repeatedly sought to cut the amount of political money spent by unions. Under earlier Republican administrations, the unions played a tempering or balancing role, but that is no longer true.

To the elderly southerners who are still the patriarchs of the religious right, such as Jerry Falwell and Pat Robertson, the unions still represent the civil rights movement of the sixties (when the white fundamentalist preachers were emphatically on the wrong side of history). Indeed, among working and middle-class families, the influence of the religious right's churches and parishes has surpassed the locals and lodges of the labor movement, which has provided both money and manpower to the Democratic Party from the New Deal onward. That may well be the single most important shift behind the nation's political realignment.

Both the corporate and religious Republicans also despise any attempt to improve public ethics by regulating lobbying and political expenditure—the issue that originally brought them together behind Bush and against McCain in 2000, according to former Christian Coalition lobbyist Marshall Wittmann.

"The alliance of Mammon and the religious right was consummated in opposition to McCain's support for campaign finance reform," recalls Wittmann, who worked for Ralph Reed on Capitol Hill as the coalition's legislative director until he became disillusioned. "When I was at the Christian Coalition, I witnessed firsthand the alliance of the deregulation, no-tax crowd with the religious conservatives. Ironically, the rank and file of the religious right are hardly the country club set. They are largely middle-class Americans who don't rely on trust funds or dividend checks for their livelihoods.

"But the leaders of the religious right have betrayed their constituents by failing to champion such economic issues as family leave or access to health insurance, which would relieve the stresses on many working families. The only things the religious conservatives get are largely symbolic votes on proposals guaranteed to fail, such as the gay marriage constitutional amendment. The religious right has consistently provided the ground troops, while the big-money men have gotten the goodies."

According to Wittmann, who eventually resigned in disgust to work for McCain, "The realization that the religious right had essentially become a front for the moneymen of the Republican Party was a primary source of my disenchantment with that movement. And without a doubt, the GOP has merely become a vehicle for unbridled corporate power."

Randy Brinson, an Alabama physician who organized Redeem the Vote, the largest evangelical voter-registration drive in recent years, has expressed dissatisfaction with the Republican corporate bias. In an interview with the *Washington Monthly*, he complained, "The power structure in the Republican Party is too entrenched with big business. It's not with evangelicals— they're a means to an end. . . . Can't they see that Republicans are just pandering to them?"

WHATEVER CONTRADICTIONS AND tensions exist between the religious right and the corporate lobby—over such intractable problems as immigration, for example—they continue to be outweighed by their shared objectives and mutual control of the Republican Party. Each side may believe that it is using the other, and both may have reason to think so. The theocratic, dominionist ideology of the religious right and the corrupting money of the corporate lobbyists continue to threaten democratic self-government. Their combined power continues to make that threat formidable, particularly when arrayed behind a messianic president who believes that he is inspired by God and empowered to rule without constitutional constraints. As traditional conservatives have begun to realize, this brand of politics is neither traditional nor conservative—and is increasingly hard to recognize as American.

FIVE

THE REVENGE
OF NIXON'S HEIRS

If in the opinion of the people the distribution or modification of
the constitutional powers be in any particular wrong, let it be
corrected by an amendment in the way which the Constitution
designates. But let there be no change by usurpation; for though
this in one instance may be the instrument of good, it is the customary weapon by which free governments are destroyed.
> —GEORGE WASHINGTON, *Farewell Address*, September 17, 1796

Well, when the president does it that means it is not illegal.
> —RICHARD M. NIXON, discussing the limits of presidential power
> with television interviewer David Frost, May 19, 1977

The President is always right.
> —DEPUTY ATTORNEY GENERAL STEVEN BRADBURY, testifying before the Senate
> Judiciary Committee, making what he later said was a "humorous" remark, July 11, 2006

LIVING IN BITTER exile after his forced resignation, Richard Milhous Nixon could hardly have foreseen that some-day another generation of Republican politicians would seek to vindicate his authoritarian vision of executive power—or that they would be led by men who had once worked on his staff and campaign. The pedigree of the Bush administration and its most fervent ideological supporters leads directly back to Nixon's unla-mented presidency—as do their pretexts for expanding presiden-tial power in the direction of dictatorship

Invocations of Nixon long ago became a cheap currency in American political culture, so devalued as to be nearly devoid of real meaning. During the years since his death even conserva-tive Republicans have occasionally uttered "Nixonian" as a term of abuse against a Democrat (usually Bill Clinton). By the time he left office in 1974, the great majority of citizens understood that he and his right-wing mafia had perverted the electoral pro-cess, the law enforcement system, and government itself in a manner the nation had not seen before. But historical amnesia is a disabling disease of our political culture. Most Americans, even those who lived through the Nixon era, have forgotten the context—let alone the details—of the Watergate scandal. That context is in many ways essential to understanding our present condition.

It is important to note here that Nixon also sought to expand presidential power in ways that were neither secret nor criminal but still threatening to the constitutional balance of power.

Broadly speaking, he dismissed congressional authority by impounding funds appropriated for purposes he didn't approve, and reorganizing the federal government without consulting the legislature that had created those departments and agencies. He circumvented Congress in his conduct of war in Vietnam and Cambodia, committing acts that almost became an additional count in the impeachment resolution before he resigned.

In all those aspects, the Bush regime descends directly from the Nixon Republicans. So does the line of argument that the nation's most powerful officials have used to justify an unprecedented aggrandizement of unaccountable power. The parallels are striking, but the difference is that Bush, Cheney, and Rove, and the forces they represent, are far more developed and powerful than the Nixon gang ever was.

Dangerous, vengeful, and felonious as he had been at the zenith of his power, Nixon in hindsight sounded almost naïve explaining himself to interviewer David Frost during a 1977 public television appearance. Amid the turmoil of protest against the war in Vietnam, with scores of bombings, violent demonstrations and even more violent revolutionary rhetoric, not to mention urban rioting and a militant black power movement rising in the ghettos, the embattled president conflated the protesters with his own political adversaries. Hostile newspapers that had published classified secrets of the Vietnam conflict hidden in the Pentagon Papers, Eastern "elites" associated with the Kennedy family and the Ivy League, liberals (and especially liberal Jews) in the universities, the media, and the government, dissenting figures in his own administration—all stimulated his innate paranoia. Identifying his presidency with the American state, he saw both threatened by these remorseless enemies. In defense of nation and presidency, any action was legitimate: "When the president does it . . ."

The register of indictments against the Nixon gang ranged

from wiretapping, burglaries, infiltrations of antiwar groups, espionage against Democratic campaigns, misuse of the Internal Revenue Service, the Central Intelligence Agency, the Federal Bureau of Investigation, and the Justice Department, and political dirty tricks of every description; to bribery, obstruction of justice, and perjury covering up those initial offenses; and all financed by illegal corporate slush funds. (At various points Nixon's henchmen—those "healthy right-wing exuberants" as he called them on the Watergate tapes—seriously contemplated the assassination of the investigative journalist Jack Anderson and the firebombing of the Brookings Institution, a moderately liberal think tank in Washington.)

These broad and varied criminal conspiracies, filed under the historical rubric of Watergate, encompassed far more than a "third-rate burglary" (in Nixon press secretary Ron Ziegler's memorable phrase).

The bungled break-in at the Democratic National Committee headquarters in the famed office and apartment complex on the Potomac came to symbolize the gangsterism of the Nixon regime. At the bottom were fascist thugs like G. Gordon Liddy, who plotted the black-bag jobs, warrantless wiretaps, illegal spying, and campaign dirty tricks, all in the cause of reelecting the president in 1972. In the middle were the white-collar types, those lawyers and bureaucrats who collected bundles of cash from corrupt corporations and then handed out the money for secret campaign slush funds and hush-money payoffs. At the top sat the president, along with his White House palace guard and his corrupted appointees at Justice, the CIA, and the FBI.

The president and his advisers, including the attorney general, became aware of these crimes and conspiracies, fully understood their illegality, and sought to conceal the evidence from the courts and Congress. But as Nixon told David Frost three years later, he did not believe that he could be held accountable for such offenses if they were committed to preserve national security.

"If the president, for example, approves something because of the national security, or in this case because of a threat to internal peace and order of significant magnitude, then the president's decision in that instance is one that enables those who carry it out, to carry it out without violating a law," he explained to Frost. Like Lincoln, who had been forced to suspend certain rights and liberties during the Civil War, he had acted to preserve the nation and the Constitution.

"This nation was torn apart in an ideological way by the war in Vietnam, as much as the Civil War tore apart the nation when Lincoln was president."

When the startled Frost asked him whether there was "anything in the Constitution . . . that suggests the president is . . . that far above the law," the former president replied with disarming candor:

"No, there isn't. There's nothing specific that the Constitution contemplates in that respect. I haven't read every word, every jot and every tittle, but I do know this: That it has been, however, argued that as far as a president is concerned, that in wartime, a president does have certain extraordinary powers which would make acts that would otherwise be unlawful, lawful if undertaken for the purpose of preserving the nation and the Constitution, which is essential for the rights we're all talking about."

In Nixon's vague formulation of an unbounded presidency could be discerned the edge of a pernicious theory that his political heirs would extend and sharpen into a formidable weapon of power.

TRACING THE LINEAL descent of the Bush administration from the Nixon White House is simple enough, and begins with the president. While George W. Bush prefers to identify himself with the sunny and popular Ronald Reagan, the truth is that the Bush family's rise in the Republican Party and national politics owed at least as much to Richard Nixon, who had been his father's first important political patron and mentor. It was Nixon who had rescued George Herbert Walker Bush from the ignominy of two failed attempts to win a Senate seat in Texas, resuscitating a career that might otherwise have ended after a few terms as a congressman from Houston.

It was Nixon who introduced the notion that Bush should be considered for higher office in 1968, short-listing the young congressman for vice president on his ticket. And it was Nixon who ensured that Bush would be taken seriously as a potential candidate for national office by appointing him to serve as United States ambassador to the United Nations and then as Republican National Committee chairman. The Nixon gang had been financially generous to Bush Senior as well, trusting him sufficiently to provide more than $100,000 in cash—from a secret slush fund known as the Townhouse account—for his 1970 Texas Senate campaign against Lloyd Bentsen.

George H. W. Bush had, in turn, promoted the fortunes of Dick Cheney, who entered government service in 1969 as a young functionary in the Nixon White House. As an extraordinarily strong and influential vice president, Cheney embodies the Nixonian vision of executive power. Taciturn and secretive, Cheney has nevertheless articulated that vision in unmistakable terms. He regards his purpose as the restoration of the untrammeled authority that Nixon sought to exercise, which was diminished by his resignation and disgrace—and by the subsequent passage of laws that restricted presidential prerogatives and opened government to public scrutiny.

To Cheney, these changes were anathema. "In thirty-four years, I have repeatedly seen an erosion of the powers and the ability of the president of the United States to do his job," he said during a television interview in January 2002. Nearly four years later, in December 2005, after the *New York Times* revealed the Bush administration's warrantless surveillance program, he told reporters: "I do have the view that over the years there had been an erosion of presidential power and authority. . . . A lot of the things around Watergate and Vietnam both, in the seventies, served to erode the authority I think the President needs . . . I believe in a strong, robust executive authority, and I think the world we live in demands it."

Echoes from that earlier era could be heard clearly by Representative Jane Harman, a California Democrat who, as the ranking minority member of the House Intelligence Committee, clashed repeatedly with Cheney and his staff. "They're focused on restoring the Nixon presidency," she told *New Yorker* reporter Jane Mayer. "They've persuaded themselves that, following Nixon, things went all wrong."

The vice president shares his autocratic convictions with Donald Rumsfeld, the defense secretary whose association with Cheney dates back to the Nixon White House. Their friendship began after Nixon appointed Rumsfeld, who had served several terms as a congressman from Illinois, to run the Office of Economic Opportunity, and Rumsfeld hired Cheney as his special assistant. Both men rose steadily on the White House staff, winning influence and credentials, with Rumsfeld eventually named as counselor to the president and Cheney as assistant to the president.

Both escaped the taint of Watergate by departing before the administration imploded. Months before the scandal broke in 1972, Nixon appointed Rumsfeld ambassador to NATO. Cheney left the White House in 1973 to work at an investment bank operated by his friend Bruce Bradley. When Gerald Ford ascended to the presidency after Nixon's resignation, he called on Rumsfeld, who had served in the House of Representatives with him, to return as his chief of staff. Rumsfeld brought back Cheney as his deputy. Within a year Ford promoted Rumsfeld to become secretary of defense, the youngest in the nation's history, and Cheney became White House chief of staff (and also the youngest ever named to that post).

Behind the fresh face of young Cheney, however, was a cynical mind-set. According to Bradley, a Republican who clearly realized the depth of Nixon's crimes, his friend had interpreted the unfolding disaster of Watergate as a partisan confrontation rather than a constitutional crisis.

"He claimed it was just a political ploy by the president's enemies," Bradley told the writer T. D. Allman decades later. "Cheney saw politics as a game where you never stop pushing. He said the presidency was like one of those giant medicine balls. If you get ahold of it, what you do is, you keep pushing that ball and you never let the other team push back."

Karl Rove, too, considered Nixon to be more a victim than a perp. As a leader of the College Republicans and an activist in the president's reelection campaign, he had worked so closely with the secret corps of dirty tricksters—notably the notorious Donald Segretti, who eventually went to prison—that he briefly drew the attention of the Watergate prosecutors, but Rove was never charged with any wrongdoing.

He had arrived in the capital by a curious route. In August 1973, exactly a year before Nixon's resignation, the *Washington Post* published a story about the twenty-two-year-old Rove headlined "RNC Probes Official as Teacher of Tricks." Evidently young Rove and another college GOP activist had been traveling across country from one campus to the next, teaching the darker arts of political warfare.

Their dirty-tricks tutorial included war stories, such as the time that Karl had stolen stationery from the campaign of Illinois

Democratic senator Alan Dixon, and printed up invitations on the letterhead to an event where there would be "free beer, free food, girls, and a good time for nothing" at Dixon's Chicago headquarters. Sent around to the city's soup kitchens, skid rows, and red-light districts, the invitations caused an embarrassing scene at the headquarters when hundreds of poor, indigent men showed up at the Dixon office on opening day.

The nasty prank hadn't done much damage. The Democrat won anyway. But somebody had taped Rove telling that story and teaching the tricks he had learned from Segretti—and then given the incriminating tape to the *Post*.

George H. W. Bush, then the chairman of the Republican National Committee, conducted an investigation of the charges against Rove, who claimed that the tape had been altered. Instead of punishing him, Bush expelled from the party a college rival of Rove, whom Bush suspected of having leaked the tape, and hired Rove to work at the party's national office in Washington. That was the beginning of his long relationship with the Bush family.

While the Watergate prosecutors never pursued any charges against him, Rove might have been intimidated by their questioning, but he wasn't. The tough, devious young operative spent the impeachment summer of 1974 in Washington, circulating pro-Nixon literature from a bogus grassroots group he set up called Americans for the Presidency, and denouncing "the lynch-mob atmosphere created in this city by the *Washington Post* and other parts of the Nixon-hating media." Like Cheney, Rove could see nothing wrong in what the ousted president had done.

For the hard right, Nixon's departure did not represent a victory for the rule of law and the Constitution, but instead the political triumph of all the forces they hated. He had asserted the Republican will to power and the ideology of conservative authoritarianism against the liberal enemy, whose names he kept on a long list. He had challenged the Congress, the courts, the media, the entire constitutional establishment. He had proven that he was willing to do anything to beat them. And he had gone down to defeat in a struggle that would be fought again when the right regained political domination—and extirpated those enemies. As a venerable conservative told author Rick Perlstein not long ago: "I never really liked Nixon *until* Watergate."

LONG BEFORE NIXON'S usurpations, Sinclair Lewis conceived the outlines of an American presidential tyranny that overthrows the constitutional order. In *It Can't Happen Here*, the presidential candidate and would-be dictator "Buzz" Windrip declares that, with America threatened by enemies domestic and foreign, traditional checks and balances are an impediment to national security. His platform includes certain drastic changes, which he carries out swiftly upon winning the election of 1936:

> Congress shall, immediately upon our inauguration, initiate amendments to the Constitution providing (a), that the President shall have the authority to institute and execute all necessary measures for the conduct of the government during this critical epoch; (b), that Congress shall serve only in an advisory capacity, calling to the attention of the President and his aides and Cabinet any needed legislation, but not acting upon same until authorized by the President so to act; and (c), that the Supreme Court shall immediately have removed from its jurisdiction the power to negate, by ruling them to be unconstitutional or by any other judicial action, any or all acts of the President, his duly appointed aides, or Congress.

Only in satire would a politician so boldly proclaim an outrageous plan for self-aggrandizement. In reality neither Nixon nor Bush ever demanded such changes in the Constitution, of course. They claimed instead to find justifications for their lawlessness in its text. Nor did they openly breach the balance of power and declare the supremacy of the president over the legislative and judicial branches. They simply behaved as if the other branches no longer mattered.

According to the original Nixonian doctrine refurbished by Republican lawyers and propagandists, America's traditional checks and balances are no longer meaningful or useful. In the name of national security—precisely the same justification employed by Nixon—the president can do whatever he deems necessary, in secret, and neither Congress nor the judiciary can hold him accountable. Now that the theory has a name—"the unitary presidency" (sometimes also called "the unitary executive")—and a cadre of determined supporters, it poses a greater threat to democratic values than it did in the early 1970s.

Eventually the Congress and the courts rose up against Nixon and threw him out before he could fully develop those arguments. But in the three decades since, an enormous organizational apparatus has grown up in and around the Republican Party, which can marshal lawyers and propaganda behind the doctrine of presidential supremacy (so long as a Republican is president). Those organizations, from the Federalist Society and the Heritage Foundation to Fox News Channel and the *Wall Street Journal*, moved in lockstep behind Cheney and Bush as they swept aside law, liberty, and tradition to implement their new order. The institutions that ought to have stood in their path often colluded or compromised with them, intimidated by the constant invocation of permanent war.

The result was to release the Bush White House from many of the normal constraints of constitutional government. According to the theories propounded by the administration's Federalist Society legal experts, such as John Yoo, the president's observance of laws passed by Congress and treaties ratified by the Senate was optional in a time of war. Bush could order illegal surveillance of American citizens, the same crime for which Nixon had been ousted, and do so with impunity. His regime could order the torture of captured Arabs and Afghans held by American forces, in violation of the Geneva conventions and the U.N. Convention Against Torture, and escape any sanctions.

John Yoo, then the deputy director of the Justice Department's Office of Legal Counsel, drafted the memoranda justifying these policies at the behest of Cheney's chief counsel (and later chief of staff) David Addington. In their view, the commander-in-chief authority vested in the president by Article II of the Constitution permitted him the latitude not only to wiretap without warrants but to void other constitutional rights and to ignore the other branches of government. "The government may be justified in taking measures which in less troubled conditions could be seen as infringements of individual liberties," he wrote.

Congress could not place any "limits on the president's determinations as to any terrorist threat, the amount of military force to be used in response, or the method, timing and nature of the response. These decisions, under our Constitution, are for the president alone to make." Nor did the president have to heed the courts, which were to defer in wartime to the executive.

The war on terror, the long war, the global struggle against violent extremism—by whatever name, this permanent war has provided more to the Bush administration than a political theme for partisan domination. Permanent war also created a durable rationale for the exercise of lawless power once exemplified by Nixon. That rationale stunned *Washington Post* columnist Jim Hoagland, usually no critic of the Bush administration, when a top White House aide explained why they felt no compunction about engaging in torture, warrantless wiretaps, and other blatantly illegal policies. The official explained:

The powers of the presidency have been eroded and usurped to the breaking point. We are engaged in a new kind of war that cannot be fought by old methods. It can only be directed by a strong executive who alone is not subject to the conflicting pressures that legislators or judges face. The public understands and supports that unpleasant reality, whatever the media and intellectuals say.

To the contrary, many public opinion surveys showed strong public disapproval of Bush's handling of the war on terror by the fifth anniversary of 9/11—but it was also true that the wave of terror scares, federal alerts, and arrests of alleged terror plotters tended to weaken public resistance to encroachments on civil liberties. Polls and elections have revealed contradictory views of how much freedom could be surrendered to purchase a modicum of security—and whether a government led by Bush can be trusted to safeguard either liberty or security.

Public opinion, however, is not an adequate measure of legitimacy for the actions of the executive in a constitutional democracy. The Constitution, as George Washington suggested in his farewell address, is not subject to amendment by executive fiat. The president is not endowed with absolute power and the capacity to ignore or break laws. Popular acceptance of dictatorial measures doesn't make them legal—and public "support" doesn't relieve the president of his culpability for breaking the law.

What the arrogant, anonymous Bush aide told Hoagland only emphasized the regime's authoritarian mind-set. Government can do anything consistent with the requirements of the permanent war, and can get away with anything so long as it can claim that the public "understands"—or is too frightened to protest. Even public approval isn't really necessary when much of what the government does can be kept secret. Most Americans were oblivious to the regime's lawbreaking until the *New York Times* began to expose the scope of its massive domestic surveillance programs in December 2005, more than a year after the electorate had an opportunity to hold Bush accountable in his last presidential election.

THE CIVIL LIBERTIES protections brushed aside so recklessly by Bush and Cheney represented a thoughtful democratic response to Nixon's abuses. In order to justify a broad and intrusive program of domestic surveillance of his critics, Nixon had acted on the assumption that students and other groups organizing against the war in Vietnam were receiving assistance from Communist governments. In June 1970, he instructed his aides to form a special task force, headed by Tom Charles Huston—a White House bureaucrat who had once led the conservative Young Americans for Freedom—to create a new domestic surveillance program.

The National Security Agency had been spying on antiwar and civil rights organizations for years by then, seeking evidence of foreign connections, but Nixon was dissatisfied with the results. (The NSA began spying on U.S. citizens from its inception in 1952 under a program code-named SHAMROCK. In the 1960s the NSA began pervasive domestic spying against critics of the government under a program called MINARET—this was in addition to the FBI's own domestic spying initiative known as COINTELPRO, which ran from 1956 to 1971.) Huston's new task force came up with a more ambitious program, known now as the Huston Plan, that proposed (in the words of his memo) "clearly illegal" surveillance activities ranging from bugging and mail opening to wiretapping of domestic and international telephone calls. The spying eventually expanded from the bugging of antiwar activists to surveillance of journalists and even staff members on Nixon's own National Security Council suspected of leaking to the press—and ultimately to spying on Democratic politicians considered a threat to Nixon's reelection in 1972. The greatest technical capacity for intrusive surveillance was wielded by the National Security Agency, the Pentagon behemoth that could detect and record almost any signal transmission by telephone, telegraph, satellite, or cable in the world.

The revelations about the Huston Plan and other such Orwellian programs prompted Congress to pass a series of reforms, including the Privacy Act of 1974, which strictly regulated the government's collection and use of information about private citizens, and the Foreign Intelligence Surveillance Act of 1978, or FISA, which was directed at the FBI, CIA, NSA, and Defense Department. The FISA statute, signed by President Jimmy Carter, was carefully designed to guard against abuses without hindering the surveillance necessary to protect the nation against spies and terrorists. If anything, FISA's authors bent to accommodate the needs of the intelligence community.

Whenever government agents wanted to monitor telephone conversations or other electronic communications originating in the United States, FISA required them to seek a warrant from a special Foreign Intelligence Surveillance Court—whose deliberations are conducted in strict secrecy. Created to oversee the most sensitive counterintelligence activities, the court approves wiretaps and other surveillance methods in cases where government agencies can show that their activities are meant to stop espionage, foreign conspiracies against the United States, and international terrorist activities. Obviously, the person or persons to be monitored are not able to contest the proceedings of the FISA court, as it is known, and neither can anyone else.

The FISA court has rejected far less than one-tenth of one percent of all the applications made by the government: In the more than 18,000 known cases, the FISA judges have issued only five refusals to authorize surveillance. On the extremely unusual occasions when a FISA court judge turns down a wiretap request, the government can appeal to yet another secret forum, the Foreign Intelligence Special Court of Review (or FISCOR), which rejects such requests even more rarely. Moreover, the government can begin a wiretap seventy-two hours— and in certain cases even longer—before obtaining FISA court approval.

The question of how and whether the Bush administration was observing FISA restrictions in the war on terror arose during the debate over the USA Patriot Act (2001), which had loosened some of the law's protections. In April 2004, the president went out of his way at a town hall meeting to reassure worried citizens that his government was respecting their rights.

"Now, by the way," he drawled, "any time you hear the United States government talking about wiretap, it requires—a wiretap requires a court order. Nothing has changed, by the way. When we're talking about chasing down terrorists, we're talking about getting a court order before we do so. It's important for our fellow citizens to understand, when you think Patriot Act, constitutional guarantees are in place when it comes to doing what is necessary to protect our homeland, because we value the Constitution." Like so many assertions by the president, that was a lie. As he knew when he said it, his administration had instituted a broad program of warrantless wiretapping within months after 9/11.

The rest of the country found out on December 16, 2005, when the *New York Times* published a front-page story revealing that, four years earlier, Bush had authorized the NSA to monitor phone calls and e-mails originating in the United States, without obtaining FISA warrants. According to the *Times*, the NSA had conducted surveillance on thousands of individuals. For the first time in a quarter century, the government had returned to intentionally listening in on Americans' communications without judicial warrants.

In the months that followed the initial revelations, reports in the *Times* and other media outlets disclosed that with the secret assistance of major United States telecommunications companies, the NSA had tapped directly into the main arteries of America's telephone and e-mail systems. Some of the information gathered by the NSA was turned over to other spy agencies, including the Defense Intelligence Agency. And contrary to the initial report—and the assertions of the government—some purely domestic communications between American citizens had been "accidentally" intercepted.

Such errors presumably did not trouble Cheney and his counsel Addington, who had insisted from the outset that the NSA not only could but should monitor domestic communications—without seeking lawful warrants. Over the protests of NSA lawyers worried about FISA's criminal penalties for warrantless domestic spying, the vice president insisted that such concerns should no longer hinder the government.

The president himself reacted angrily when the press raised questions about the legality of his actions. "To say 'unchecked power' basically is ascribing some kind of dictatorial position to the president, which I strongly reject," he retorted at a press conference following the *Times* disclosures (which he denounced as "shameful"). "The fact that we're discussing this program is helping the enemy."

He pointedly refused to delineate any limits on his own power, except those that he imposed on himself. "That's what's important for the American people to understand. I am doing what you expect me to do, and at the same time safeguarding the civil liberties of the country." He declared that the warrantless wiretapping program would continue, insolently daring the courts and Congress to try to stop him.

Five months later, in May 2006, the *National Journal* reported that Bush had quashed an internal and supposedly independent investigation of the NSA program by the Justice Department's Office of Professional Responsibility. The probe's subjects were the approval and oversight of the warrantless wiretaps by Attorney General Gonzales and his deputies. It had concluded abruptly when the president denied the necessary security clearances to the Justice attorneys conducting the investigation, forbidding their access to the program's classified documents.

Lawyers both within and outside the nation's law enforcement apparatus were shocked by this unprecedented action, but it was merely another incident in a pattern that had by then become routine. Constitutional attorney Jack Balkin explored the deeper meaning of Bush's behavior in his blog, Balkinization:

> You can have the President be the boss of everyone in the Executive Branch or who exercises executive functions. Or you can make the President immune from oversight and checking by the other branches. But you can't have both. If you have both, you don't have a system of checks and balances. You have a system that produces corruption, mismanagement, abuse of power and tyranny.

To lend a veneer of respectability to his boss's crude trespasses, Attorney General Gonzales tried to marshal a substantive legal defense, without much success. His thin arguments for the NSA program, articulated to the public and at congressional hearings, contradicted each other as well as history. The first argument suggested that Congress had given the president the necessary authority. The second claimed that he didn't need congressional approval because such powers are inherent in the presidency, and that any attempt by Congress to limit those powers, such as FISA, were by definition unconstitutional.

Specifically, Gonzales pointed to the Authorization to Use Military Force (AUMF), a joint resolution passed by the House and Senate on September 18, 2001—exactly a week after 9/11—which authorized Bush "to use all necessary and appropriate force against those nations, organizations, or persons" involved in the attacks, "to prevent any future acts of international terrorism against the United States." They interpreted the statute to include any and all forms of surveillance of foreign or domestic "persons" who might be connected with al Qaeda.

But there was not a word in the very brief text of the AUMF that enabled Bush to ignore the laws governing wiretapping. There was no evidence that Congress intended to void the FISA statute or other constitutional protections. Gonzales admitted that in the fall of 2001, not long after passage of the AUMF, the White House had considered seeking amendments to FISA—but had learned from certain members of Congress that passing such amendments would be difficult if not impossible. He did not explain how Congress could have intended to void a statute that he says it would not consider amending.

Should such contorted logic fail to persuade, Gonzales had a simpler answer. Under Article II of the Constitution, which names the president commander in chief of the armed forces, he can do whatever he deems necessary in time of war without the approval of Congress or the courts. So to whatever degree a law like FISA limits those inherent powers, it is unconstitutional. The attorney general went further when he appeared before the Senate Judiciary Committee in February 2006 to defend the president's actions. Asked whether the president might have the power to order wiretaps on communications between Americans within the United States, he replied, "I'm not going to rule it out." If the president indeed has inherent authority to supersede laws passed by Congress in wartime, then he would also possess the power to install wiretaps wherever and whenever he wishes.

In a state of permanent war, according to this theory, there are virtually no limitations on a president of the United States. Whatever he does to thwart terrorism is by definition legal. There can be no effective checks on him because he and his appointees and agents determine—in absolute secrecy—whose civil rights and liberties should be abrogated. That is the doctrine of the unitary presidency, which Nixon tried to articulate and which Bush and Cheney have restored.

TO CHALLENGE THE administration's radical theory, of course, was to invite Republican accusations of fecklessness and even disloyalty. Karl Rove responded to critics with his usual blend of deception, demagoguery, and opportunism. "Let me be as clear as I can: President Bush believes if al Qaeda is calling somebody in America, it is in our national security interest to know who they're calling and why," he said in a speech to the winter meeting of the Republican National Committee in January 2006. "Some important Democrats clearly disagree." As the presidential deputy well knew, no Democrat—and in fact nobody at all—had ever suggested that the government should not monitor al Qaeda's telephone calls to anybody in America or anywhere else. He knew that criticism of the NSA wiretaps had focused on the president's arrant dismissal of the laws governing surveillance and his overweening claims of power and authority not granted by the Constitution.

Rove's attacks were mild compared with the cries of treason that echoed from talk radio across the country. On television and in her syndicated column, Ann Coulter repeatedly called for the editors of the *New York Times* to be prosecuted and sent before a firing squad. San Francisco radio host Melanie Morgan, whose station maintains close ties with local Republican Party officials, urged that *Times* executive editor Bill Keller be hanged or electrocuted "after a trial." All critics of the Bush administration were subject to this kind of abuse from the nation's authoritarian entertainers, whose demand for conformity has grown in intensity and volume ever since the debate over the invasion of Iraq. Just as skeptics of the war had been branded as supporters of Saddam Hussein, so those who questioned the conduct of the permanent war were slandered as sympathizers of terrorism.

Dissenting critics would be blamed, warned Rush Limbaugh, when terrorists strike the United States again:

> Let me tell you something, folks, if we are hit again, if we are hit again, we need to hold these people in our country who are undermining our efforts responsible. It ain't going to be the FBI's fault next time. It isn't going to be the CIA's fault next time. It isn't going to be some bureaucracy's fault next time. It's going to be the fault of politicians, left-wing groups and the like who have names and identities and spend their every waking moment trying to obstruct our ability to secure intelligence information for our own national security.

"You want some names?" Limbaugh proceeded to name six Democratic senators, along with "*Newsweek, Time,* the *New York Times,* [and] Amnesty International. If we get hit again, these are the names of the people and organizations we need to look at when we're trying to find out why and how it happened."

Bill O'Reilly has repeatedly accused the American Civil Liberties Union of aiding al Qaeda by bringing lawsuits to expose and remedy the excesses of the Bush administration. "They're terrorists," he shrieked on his Fox News show. "They're terrorizing me and my family!"

Frank Gaffney, the neoconservative defense analyst who operates an industry-funded think tank, urged a limit on dissent in a book that outlines the "steps America must take to prevail in the war for the free world." In the afterword he writes, "No more praise for those who dissent. When they ask, 'Wouldn't you fight for my right to dissent?' I have to answer, 'Not right now.'" To the neoconservatives, saving the free world doesn't necessarily mean defending actual freedom.

Behind these shrill warnings and partisan accusations from the Republican right was the dubious assumption that domestic spying is directed exclusively at the nation's enemies. Yet with checks and balances swept away, and with the president as the nation's unitary leader, there was no way to be sure that the "terrorist wiretapping program," as the Republicans prefer to call it, would always be so limited. Any official as savvy and senior as Rove certainly knew better.

THE DIMENSIONS OF the domestic spying operations approved by Bush and Cheney, without congressional or judicial sanction, remain unknown. But the scope of the scandal has continued to grow steadily during the year since the initial *New York Times* exposé to a point that almost defies comprehension. Five months after that first story, *USA Today* reported that the NSA had been compiling the telephone records of millions of American citizens into an enormous secret database, with the cooperation of AT&T, Verizon, and BellSouth.

Like the warrantless wiretapping program, this effort, too, was undertaken without benefit of any judicial sanction, perhaps because no judge would have permitted it. Not only did this program manifestly flout the Fourth Amendment's requirement for probable cause, which would have been impossible to demonstrate while invading the privacy of millions of Americans, but it also violated a 1986 law known as the Stored Communications Act, which expressly forbids telephone companies to provide data to government agencies without a court order.

In response to that second embarrassing story, the Bush administration promised innocent citizens that nobody was actually listening in to their phone calls or misusing their phone records. The collection of database information was only to be used to trace calling patterns that might lead to terrorist cells. But that supposed reassurance indicated that the government was in fact planning still deeper intrusions into what had once been zones of personal privacy. The extent of the NSA program is certainly far larger than what journalists have uncovered to date. A former NSA employee named Russell Tice told the House Government Reform Committee that while working for the agency, he was concerned about a "special access" electronic surveillance program far broader than warrantless wire-tapping. More than that Tice was forbidden to say. But phone records are merely a single element in an expanding universe of information to be used by government agencies—and private contractors—for data mining.

The truly mind-boggling objective of these programs is to compile a database that includes everything about everyone—and to invent algorithms that can trace patterns to identify criminals and terrorists within the abstract universe of bits and bytes.

If such an ambitious concept seems familiar, that could be due to its close resemblance to the spooky-sounding Total Information Awareness project, which crashed and burned (or at least went into hiding) under intense publicity in late 2002. Housed in the Pentagon's ultra-high-tech Defense Advanced Research Projects Agency, the TIA program was directed by John Poindexter, the retired navy admiral, former national security adviser to President Reagan, and Iran-Contra criminal defendant. By then he was a strange choice for a sensitive government position.

When he ran the National Security Council, Poindexter had supervised the secret arms-for-hostages sales to the mullahs in terror-sponsoring Tehran and then approved the transfer of profits from those sales to the Nicaraguan Contras, despite a federal law barring government funding of the rebel force. He also shredded the evidence of the Iran-Contra scheme and lied to Congress about it. In 1990, a federal jury convicted him of perjury and obstruction of justice. But he escaped prison when his conviction was overturned on what conservatives usually call a technicality by hard-right Republican appellate judges Laurence Silberman and David Sentelle, who ruled that the case against him had depended on information provided by the defendant while testifying under a grant of congressional immunity.

Evidently the Bush administration thought Poindexter had paid his debt to society and—leaving aside the perjury, document shredding, and trading with terrorists—would provide ideal leadership to its Information Awareness project. Press secretary Ari Fleischer unwittingly demonstrated the regime's contempt for the law in defending his appointment: "Admiral Poindexter is somebody who this administration thinks is an outstanding American, an outstanding citizen, who has done a very good job in what he has done for our country, serving the military."

What Poindexter was doing for the country was aptly symbolized by his project's symbol, an occult pyramid topped by an all-seeing eye, gazing upon a globe—and its motto, "Knowledge is power." His goal was to create a gigantic matrix to track enemies of the state by amassing and analyzing every last speck of data in cyberspace, from electronic tolls to Orbitz tickets to motel charges and far more. When a Pentagon bureaucrat like Poindexter says "everything," he means literally every income tax return, every medical record, every telephone bill, every credit report, every bank-card swipe, every movie ticket, every book, and everything else that isn't paid for in cash, plus every e-mail sent by anybody anywhere.

Or as Poindexter put it, TIA would ultimately empower intelligence agencies to access "the worldwide, distributed, legacy databases as if they were one centralized database." He also promised "to develop privacy protection technologies," although neither he nor anyone else has ever explained how privacy is compatible with an omniscient centralized data repository.

This overweening scheme raised alarms from critics left to right, and none louder than William Safire, the old libertarian Republican who warned in the *New York Times* that Poindexter would soon exercise unprecedented power to invade every citizen's privacy. Actually, Poindexter and his colleagues were developing a prototype system that was not quite ready to mount the final Orwellian invasion of everyone's personal space. But TIA certainly aimed to breach all boundaries between commercial and governmental information systems, wiping out the distinction between public and private to an extent that was difficult to imagine.

In October 2003, more than a year after the program and Poindexter's role in overseeing it were revealed, Congress voted to defund the Information Awareness Office. Bush signed the legislation. The all-seeing eye was closed, at least as far as "Americans on American soil" were concerned, according to Senator Ron Wyden, the Democrat who led the effort to end TIA.

But, of course, the Bush administration wasn't about to close a spy program just because Congress told them to do so. The same work, performed by the same consultants and scientists, was simply moved to another agency—the Advanced Research and Development Activity (ARDA), based at Fort Meade, Maryland, in the headquarters of the NSA. The program's scary title and ominous symbol was scrapped for a friendlier name. "We will be describing this new effort as 'Basketball,'" explained Poindexter's partner, Brian Sharkey, who continued to oversee construction of a prototype system, in a memo to subcontractors. By late 2004, the prototype was reportedly being tested at a secret ARDA facility.

Basketball is by no means the only attempt to build a datamining doomsday machine. Intelligence sources have informed

Newsweek that Total Information Awareness was in fact renamed Topsail, and that the work went on quietly despite the uproar over Poindexter. In the *Washington Post*, military affairs columnist William Arkin named dozens of programs, including Basketball and Topsail, whose costs and details are concealed in the multi-billion-dollar classified budgets of the Pentagon, the Department of Homeland Security, and the intelligence agencies. Run mostly by private consulting companies, these data-mining experiments aim to improve the government's capacity to compile, sort, and instantly extract information from the vast cyber environment that now surrounds and defines every citizen.

The implications are clear to Arkin, a former army intelligence analyst who has long been among the most astute observers of the U.S. defense establishment. "Although there is no evidence that the harvesting programs have been involved in illegal activity or have been abused to reach into the lives of innocent Americans," he wrote, "their sheer scope, the number of 'transactions' being tracked, raises questions as to whether an all-seeing domestic surveillance system isn't slowly being established, one that in just a few years' time will be able to reveal the interactions of any targeted individual in near real time."

WHILE AMERICA AWAITS the completion of the "total information" police state, old-fashioned methods of surveillance and harassment must suffice to intimidate dissent. The theories and aspirations of the Republican regime are more sophisticated than those once employed by Nixon, but many of the techniques remain the same. The Bush administration and its aggressive advocates insist that only terrorists need fear the long arm of the unitary presidency, but its reach apparently extends well beyond any actual threat.

It would be easier to believe that Bush's wiretapping and surveillance programs are aimed solely at terrorists and their allies if there were not so much evidence already of Nixonian abuses by his administration.

In December 2005, the same month that the *New York Times* first reported the existence of the NSA's warrantless wiretaps, NBC News broke an equally disturbing story that received much less attention. The Pentagon had established a secret domestic counterintelligence program, known as TALON, to gather "non-validated threat information and security anomalies indicative of possible terrorist pre-attack activity." What that bit of jargon meant in practice, according to documents obtained by NBC and *Newsweek*, was monitoring peace groups and other political groups deemed hostile to the administration. In TALON's database files were thousands of pages of dossiers devoted to antiwar meetings and protests.

The pretext for compiling this database of dissenters was that they might pose a threat to the Defense Department's installations and personnel, although there was no evidence that the protest groups had contemplated any violent or illegal action. As part of the "terrorism threat warning process," the TALON investigators filed reports on peaceful protests, including an antiwar rally at Hollywood and Vine streets in Los Angeles, a gathering at a Quaker meeting in Lake Worth, Florida, and an anticorruption demonstration at the headquarters of the Halliburton Corporation in Houston, Texas.

These innocuous events, and many others like them, are stigmatized in Pentagon files as "suspicious incidents" that might pose a threat to national security. Documents obtained by NBC showed that TALON investigated forty-three antiwar events between November 2004 and May 2005, with agents filing reports from Washington, D.C., Arizona, Arkansas, California, Colorado, Connecticut, Florida, Georgia, Illinois, Louisiana, Massachusetts, Nebraska, New Jersey, New York, North Carolina,

Ohio, Pennsylvania, Rhode Island, Texas, Vermont, and Wisconsin.

An elderly protester named Gail Sredanovic, who belongs to an antiwar organization called the Raging Grannies, told journalists that she regarded the federal gumshoes with disdain. "Aside from the disturbing civil liberties aspects of the Pentagon spying on local peace groups, it makes me scared to think that the folks in charge of protecting us from possible terrorist attacks can't tell the difference between a terrorist threat and a peaceful citizen gathering," she said. "Are they really that stupid?"

The short answer is yes, they are. Not so coincidentally, the TALON program had been instituted in May 2003—just as the invasion of Iraq was completed—on orders from Paul Wolfowitz, the war's chief architect and then deputy defense secretary. The TALON operations belonged to a secretive wing of the Pentagon known as Counterintelligence Field Activity, or CIFA, which the Bush administration has sought to transform into a secret military police agency with broad domestic powers.

Under a proposal floated by a presidential commission headed by the ubiquitous Judge Laurence Silberman, CIFA would expand its duties from those of a security agency that protects military facilities into a police agency with the authority to investigate crimes such as treason and sabotage. Silberman apparently believes that the United States lacks a sufficient panoply of secret police agencies. At the same time, the Pentagon has also proposed legislation to weaken the Privacy Act, so that the FBI can provide more information about U.S. citizens to CIFA and other defense agencies.

Citing the terrorist threat, the FBI has returned to spying on war protesters and other peaceful dissenters. Over the past few years, the American Civil Liberties Union has obtained internal documents proving that the bureau, in behavior reminiscent of the late J. Edgar Hoover, has opened investigations of Greenpeace, the worldwide environmental organization; People for the Ethical Treatment of Animals, an animal rights protest group; and the ACLU itself. The investigations of Greenpeace and PETA were supposedly aimed at potential "ecoterrorist" crimes, despite the lack of evidence of any criminal acts. According to ACLU staffers, the FBI investigators had gathered derogatory information on Greenpeace and PETA from the Washington Legal Foundation and other right-wing organizations, whose vested ideological interests were hostile to both groups.

As for the ACLU, executive director Anthony Romero sounded dumbfounded when asked about the files on his venerable organization. "I'm still somewhat shocked by the size of the file on us," said Romero. "Why would the FBI collect almost 1,200 pages on a civil rights organization engaged in lawful activity? What justification could there be, other than political surveillance of lawful First Amendment activities?"

Yet another domestic surveillance scheme, in some ways more sinister than wiretaps and data mining, has been revived by the Department of Homeland Security. Again this is a plan supposedly scrapped after public and congressional protest, only to be quietly revived by the Bush administration in a different form. In 2002, the Department of Justice attempted to recruit utility and telephone workers, cable TV installers, letter carriers, delivery drivers, and others who regularly enter private homes to enlist as federal informants. They would report suspicious persons, activities, and items that they observed, and their information would be entered into law enforcement databases. When Operation TIPS (Terrorist Information and Prevention System) was reported, the outcry against its totalitarian style was deafening. The attorney general and the president backed away from the project, whose funding was cut off by a coalition of liberal and conservative legislators.

But the Department of Homeland Security quietly resumed

implementation of the TIPS program during the winter of 2005—using school bus drivers instead of cable installers. The department expects to train tens and perhaps hundreds of thousands of drivers to watch for potential terrorists in the neighborhoods they serve. The School Bus Watch program seeks "to turn 600,000 bus drivers into an army of observers." The notion is that drivers will learn which cars belong on the streets they serve, and which are suspiciously out of place. Aside from the paranoia and false reporting that such a program will inevitably cause, it could be laughed off as a waste of federal money. What matters, however, is the mind-set of the administration—the same mind-set reflected in all of the illegal or dubious surveillance programs that the Republican regime has instigated. They are all important because they demonstrate the unilateral will of the president to use any means at his disposal, whether approved by Congress and the courts or not, and his utter determination to create a surveillance society that no longer vests any meaning in traditional ideas of freedom and privacy.

AMONG THOSE HONORED American concepts is the expectation that when individual rights are violated, citizens can seek redress from an impartial court. That right is on the verge of extinction, however, because the Bush administration is claiming the authority to quash civil litigation that might lead to the exposure of so-called state secrets. Although other presidents have used the state secrets claim in the past to stifle lawsuits that might damage national security, Bush is now deploying it to cover up his own potentially unlawful acts. In the spring and summer of 2006, the administration demanded that the federal courts dismiss three cases concerning the NSA surveillance programs. Those cases included a lawsuit by the Electronic Frontier Foundation, a nonpartisan public interest group, against

AT&T and the NSA for using secret computerized facilities to spy on the telephone company's customers; a civil rights lawsuit brought by the American Civil Liberties Union against the NSA; and a similar lawsuit brought by the Center for Constitutional Rights against the Bush administration. The ACLU case was the first to be dismissed.

The courts seemed to offer the only way to vindicate rights violated by the Republican regime, since the Senate and the House of Representatives had proved to be such pliable instruments of the White House over the past five years. Roused to occasional protest by the most egregious misconduct on the part of the president and his cabinet—such as the torture scandals in American military prisons abroad—a bipartisan Senate majority usually settled back down to doing nothing without posing any real challenge to the unitary executive.

The Senate Intelligence Committee, for example, spent more than two years avoiding a real investigation of how intelligence on Iraq was manipulated and misused by the White House, simply because the committee chairman was a pliant tool of the regime rather than the kind of self-respecting legislator contemplated by the Constitution. The same, unfortunately, could be said of most if not all of the Republican leadership in the Senate. (The House has been a completely useless institution, scarcely worth mentioning as a constitutional balance to the president. It was led by a corrupt rabble that did away with ethics oversight in favor of open boodling, pandering to corporate interests, and posturing for the party's right-wing base.)

When Senator Arlen Specter of Pennsylvania, then the chairman of the Senate Judiciary Committee, raised questions about the legality of the NSA surveillance program—and especially about the White House failure to inform Congress about its intelligence programs as mandated by law—the vice president, who is really in control, ignored and humiliated him. The noisy but abject Specter made a show of complaining, but actually responded by drafting a bill that would essentially repeal FISA and allow Bush complete latitude in domestic spying.

And in the autumn of 2006, following many months of dramatic rhetorical resistance to the president's extraordinary claim that he could order the imprisonment and abuse of anyone deemed an enemy of the state, Senators McCain, Graham, and Warner joined sixty-two of their Senate colleagues in endorsing the Military Commissions Act—a sweeping surrender of traditional rights and liberties to the unitary executive. This bill, passed by both houses and sent to the president on September 30, 2006, purported to resolve the impasse between the Bush White House and the Supreme Court over the *Hamdan* case, which became the subject of lengthy negotiations between the McCain group and the White House. But in the end, McCain and his colleagues, along with the Democratic senators who had turned their proxies over to the Arizona Republican, went along with an alleged compromise that was, in fact, an abdication of historic proportions.

The bill created a new, extra-constitutional system of militarized justice to permit the imprisonment, interrogation, trial, and punishment of individuals designated by the president as enemy combatants, outside the protections of the Bill of Rights. Under this system, the president would decide whether waterboarding and other forms of torture violated America's Geneva obligations. The president would decide to whom these methods could be applied. Those unfortunate people would have none of the rights formerly afforded them by the U.S. Constitution and the Geneva Conventions, except insofar as the president allowed, without the possibility of judicial review. The A ct abrogated all the constitutional protections and the Geneva Conventions that the dissenting senators had promised to defend.

Noting that the Democratic leadership in the Senate had

submitted against its conscience to this Act, fearing that Bush and Rove would depict any resistance as softness on terrorism, the *New York Times* did not exaggerate in an editorial on the Act's meaning, "Congress," declared the *Times*, had "passed a tyrannical law that will be ranked with the low points in American democracy, our generation's version of the Alien and Sedition Acts." Although thirty-three Democratic senators and one Republican had voted nay, the authoritarian White House had been able to rely on its own partisans and the red-state Democrats most frightened of right-wing retribution.

No wonder the president has felt free to ignore the will of the legislative branch, accepting their bills pro forma—and then sending back "signing statements" that explain why he is disinclined to obey the laws they pass. As the *Boston Globe* revealed in a pathbreaking analysis in April 2006, Bush has appended statements questioning the constitutionality of more than 750 laws sent down from Capitol Hill for his signature. While he has vetoed only one bill—as provided by the Constitution for bills that he believes are unconstitutional or unwise—he has used the signing statements to assert his own supremacy. While other presidents have occasionally used such statements, Bush has done so far more aggressively than his predecessors, according to presidential scholars.

In some instances, he has essentially declined to enforce or obey a law because he believes doing so would "impair foreign relations, the national security, the deliberative processes of the Executive, or the performance of the Executive's constitutional duties." In other cases, Bush has eerily echoed the Buzz Windrip doctrine of a Congress stripped of its constitutional authority— with a signing statement saying he regards a duly passed statute not as a law that his administration must obey, but as an advisory opinion with no force. The Senate has whined about the signing statements but has done nothing. Only the nation's highest court, divided as it is along ideological lines, has displayed any will to resist the domineering machinations of this president and vice president, their Federalist Society lawyers, and the authoritarian Republicans in Congress. The most important constitutional vindication in recent years came in late June 2006, when five justices ruled against the Bush administration in *Hamdan v. Rumsfeld.*

The majority opinion written by Justice John Paul Stevens briskly rejected the theories of Cheney, Addington, Yoo, and Gonzales as to the plenary powers of the president in wartime. The president must comply with statutes and treaties approved by Congress, and he is not relieved of that duty by his status as commander in chief. Those statutes require the president and his subordinates to comply with the laws of war and the Geneva Conventions, especially with regard to torture and other abusive interrogation techniques. The president cannot unilaterally deprive citizens of their rights to due process. And the Supreme Court, unlike the supine members of the Senate and House, reiterated its own coequal status as a constitutional partner with the other branches.

In a concurring opinion, Justice Anthony Kennedy made the same points even more clearly. Both his and the Stevens opinion clearly rebuffed White House claims that the president had been granted additional powers by the Authorization to Use Military Force—the same argument that Gonzales had used to justify the NSA spying program. If the AUMF had not given Bush the authority to convene military commissions to try prisoners of war, in direct violation of other existing statutes and treaties, then it had not given him the authority to abrogate domestic laws governing surveillance, either.

The *Hamdan* decision also rejected the argument that Article II of the Constitution somehow conferred special discretion on the president to disobey statutes such as FISA. In a footnote to the *Hamdan* decision, the court explicitly disallowed that arrogant claim: "Whether or not the President has independent power, absent congressional authorization, to convene military commissions, he may not disregard limitations that Congress has, in proper exercise of its own war powers, placed on his powers."

But the *Hamdan* decision was by no means unanimous. Chief Justice John Roberts had ruled against Hamdan while sitting on the appellate bench, which no doubt had been an important reason for his nomination to the Supreme Court. (In fact some observers wondered whether Roberts should not have recused himself from the *Hamdan* case in the appellate court, since he was known to be a candidate for promotion by the White House—the defendant in that case.) There was in any event no doubt about his views on the subject of presidential powers. His recusal when *Hamdan* came before the Supreme Court left the right-wing brethren—Justices Antonin Scalia, Clarence Thomas, and Samuel Alito—to side with the administration.

In their respective debuts, both Roberts and Alito have proved that their promises of moderation while seeking Senate confirmation were hollow. Along with Thomas and to a lesser degree Scalia, the new justices are exponents of the unitary executive and the untrammeled power of the president in wartime.

While Alito sought to soften his position during the hearings on his nomination, he delivered a speech to the Federalist Society's national convention in November 2000 that endorsed the most extreme perspective. The Constitution, he told his fellow ideologues, "makes the President the head of the executive branch, but it does more than that. The President has not just some executive powers, but *the* executive power—the whole thing." Although he told the Senate Judiciary Committee that the president is not above the law, that bland reassurance was meaningless because under the extreme Federalist version of the unitary presidency, the president's will *is* the law. Alito has also been an advocate of presidential signing statements since he worked in the Reagan White House more than two decades ago.

With few exceptions, Scalia has been a staunch advocate of the expansion of presidential authority ever since his earliest jobs in Nixon's Office of Legal Counsel and as an assistant attorney general under President Ford. As for Thomas, the least independent and thoughtful member of the court, he is expected to vote reliably with the other three conservatives. In 2004, he was willing to surrender the Supreme Court's own powers, arguing that he and his fellow justices were prohibited from ruling on the Bush administration's mistreatment of war prisoners at Guantánamo.

The ultimate triumph for Bush, his party, and any future leader who shares his philosophy of permanent war and presidential aggrandizement would be the Supreme Court's stamp of approval on his unsurpations. It is possible that the future of democratic governance in America will be determined in the final two years of the Bush presidency, when the Republicans may yet secure a court majority that reinterprets the Constitution as a mandate for theocratic dominion and untrammeled presidential power. That would raise the real prospect of an authoritarian regime acting under color of the Constitution and the law while eviscerating both. The first long step in that direction has already been taken with the Military Commissions Act, whose blatant assault on legal traditions, constitutional rights, and judicial authority must eventually be confronted by the high court.

In the winter of 2006, only months after the successful appointments of Roberts and Alito, the right-wing media began to agitate for the retirement of Stevens, who is eighty-six years old and the court's most liberal member. Should he or any of the four justices on the liberal side die or retire, the Senate will have to rediscover its courage, its willingness to filibuster, and its purpose as the national bulwark against a radical faction such as the authoritarian Republicans.

Certainly that was the role envisioned for the Senate by the nation's founders when they wrote the Constitution. The Democrats who won control of the upper chamber again in November 2006, however narrowly, will have the chance to fulfill that responsibility in the final two years of the Bush presidency. They can begin by seeking to amend the Military Commissions Act, as Senators Christopher Dodd of Connecticut and Patrick Leahy of Vermont have proposed, and restoring the rights of due process and the international treaty obligations of the United States. If that effort succeeds, despite the resistance of Republicans and some fellow Democrats, they will have brought the nation back from the brink of authoritarian rule.

During the past six years, however, the Republican leadership in the White House and the Congress have taken us closer and closer to a kind of government that the founders abhorred. Manipulating our fears, stirring religious divisions, and contriving to create a state of permanent war, they have sought to institute a rule by men instead of the rule of law—and they have reinvented the president as a sovereign monarch rather than an executive with limited powers. With the backing of corporate wealth and fundamentalist religion, the unitary presidency represents a potential tyranny.

Yes, it can happen here. Whether it ever will depends on our determination to defend our rights, our liberties, and our democratic inheritance, not only for ourselves but for generations to come.

NOTES

INTRODUCTION

The most important sources for the introduction are the recently reissued paperback edition of *It Can't Happen Here*, by Sinclair Lewis (New York: New American Library, 2005) and Mark Schorer's masterful biography, *Sinclair Lewis: An American Life* (New York: McGraw-Hill, 1961).

3 Lewis referred to the entire topic somewhat contemptuously as "it": Schorer, p. 608.

3 he cranked out the pages . . . in a three-month summer sprint: Schorer, p. 608.

4 sold more than 300,000 copies: Schorer, p. 610.

5 "Professional Common Man": Lewis, p. 71.

6 "a crook or a religious fanatic": Lewis, p. 124.

7 eventually brought before a military tribunal: Lewis, p. 304.

8 to use his fame and skills in the service: Schorer, p. 610.

9 powerful figures in the corporate elite and the Republican Party: See George Seldes, *Facts and Fascism* (New York: In Fact, Inc., 1943); and Jules Archer, *The Plot to Seize the White House* (New York: Hawthorn Books, 1973).

12 Barr . . . has joined the American Civil Liberties Union: Jesse Walker, "Bob Barr, Civil Libertarian," *Reason*, December 2003.

13 "a totalitarian type regime": Barr radio interview with Alex Jones, December 11, 2005, http://www.prisonplanet.com/articles/december 2005/111205totalitariandanger.htm.

13 "main components of a police state": Paul Craig Roberts, "The Police State Is Closer Than You Think," *Counterpunch.org*, October 8, 2005.

13 "a clear and present danger": Bruce Fein, ". . . unlimited?", *Washington Times*, December 20, 2005.

13 "monarchical doctrine": *Washington Post*, February 16, 2006.

1. THE "POST-9/11 WORLDVIEW" OF KARL ROVE

18 "a warning about what all modern societies were in danger of becoming": See Diana Trilling's review, "Fiction in Review," in *The Nation*, March 14, 1949; and Eric Fromm's afterword to the 1961 Signet paperback edition of *1984*, as reprinted in the Plume edition (New York: Penguin Putnam, 1983).

18 Holding forth in a cabinet meeting, Sarason "demanded: Lewis, p. 346.

19 "From a marketing point of view": Elisabeth Bumiller, "Bush Aides Set Strategy to Sell Policy on Iraq," *New York Times*, September 7, 2002.

19 the alleged facts justifying war "had been fixed": Michael Smith, "Blair Planned Iraq War from Start, *Sunday Times* (London), May 1, 2005.

21 "the post-9/11 worldview": Dan Balz, "Rove Offers Republicans a Battle Plan for Elections," *Washington Post*, January 21, 2006.

22 "We want America to speak with one voice": "Bush Urges Americans to Be 'Resolute' in New War on Terrorism," Knight-Ridder News service, September 21, 2001.

22 Norquist . . . who has known and worked with Rove: Susan Page, "Norquist Power High, Profile Low," *USA Today*, June 1, 2001.

23 he addressed the annual dinner of the New York State Conservative Party: "Remarks of Karl Rove at the New York Conservative Party," *washingtonpost.com*, June 24, 2005.

26 "the driving force behind the new slogan": Fred Kaplan, "Say G-WOT?", *Slate*, July 26, 2005.

26 it is really World War IV: Norman Podhoretz, "How to Win World War IV," *Commentary*, February 2002.

26 "the long war": http://www.defenselink.mil/qdr/.

27 He would approach other countries: http://www.pbs.org/newshour/bb/politics/july-dec00/for-policy 10-12.html.

28 "It was all about finding a way to do it": Ron Suskind, *The Price of Loyalty: George W. Bush, the White House, and the Education of Paul O'Neill* (New York, Simon & Schuster, 2004), p. 86.

28 Many of the key advisers: See Project for a New American Century Web site, notably http://www.newamericancentury.org/statementof-principles.htm.

29 Mickey Herskowitz, a Bush family confidant: Russ Baker, "Why George Went to War," *TomPaine.com*, June 20, 2005.

30 "There's a luscious double trap": John Podhoretz, "October Surprise, Please," *New York Post*, July 16, 2002.

32 "There was a perceptible shift in attitude": Michael Smith, op. cit., *Sunday Times* (London), May 1, 2005.

33 Her only lasting contribution: Patt Derian, "How to Make Dictators Look Good," *The Nation*, February 9, 1985.

34 "Kirkpatrick openly endorsed": Iain Guest, *Behind the Disappearances: Argentina's Dirty War Against Human Rights and the United Nations* (Philadelphia: University of Pennsylvania Press, 1990), p. 339–41.

35 truth alone might not always suffice: William Kristol, "From Truth to Deception," *Washington Post*, October 12, 2002.

36 The notes of a secret meeting: Richard Norton-Taylor, "Bush-Blair Deal Before Iraq War Revealed in Secret Memo," *Guardian*, February 3, 2006.

36 Paul Craig Roberts warned: "A Reckless Path," *Washington Times*, March 20, 2003.

37–38 Over the years his name has frequently surfaced in twilight intrigues: Jonathan Kwitny, "Tale of Intrigue: How an Italian Ex-Spy Who Also Helped U.S. Landed in Prison Here," *Wall Street Journal*, August 7, 1985; and Lawence E. Walsh, *Firewall: The Iran-Contra Conspiracy and Coverup* (New York: Norton, 1997), p. 43.

38 Yet on more than one occasion: Duane R. Clarridge, *A Spy for All Seasons: My Life in the CIA* (New York: Scribner, 1997) pp. 187–89.

38 the bombing of the Bologna train station: Associated Press, "Four Get Life in Prison in Bombing in Bologna," *New York Times*, July 12, 1988.

38 More recently, Ledeen has been suspected: Craig Unger, "The War They Wanted, the Lies They Needed," *Vanity Fair*, July 2006.

39 Since September 11, 2001, the busy Ledeen: Laura Rosen and Jeet Heer, "The Front," *American Prospect*, April 2005.

40 In an interview with journalist Robert Dreyfuss: Robert Dreyfuss, "Just the Beginning," *American Prospect*, April 2003.

40 He has called for total war: Michael A. Ledeen, "We'll Win This War," *American Enterprise*, December 2001.

40 For Ledeen this ominous conflagration: Michael A. Ledeen, *The War Against the Terror Masters* (New York: Truman Talley Books, 2002), p. 213.

40 Shortly after the war began: Thomas B. Edsall and Dana Milbank, "White House's Roving Eye for Politics; President's Most Powerful Adviser May Also Be the Most Connected," *Washington Post*, March 31, 2003.

Notes

40 Among his early books: Michael Ledeen with Renzo de Felice, *Fascism: An Informal Introduction to Its Theory and Practice* (New Brunswick, N.J.: Transaction Books, 1976).

41 The controversial de Felice: Richard Owen, "Italy Learns to Love Il Duce Once More," *Times* (London), November 21, 2003.

41 Ledeen's rhetoric takes on a menacing tone: Jeet Heer and Dave Wagner, "Man of the World: Michael Ledeen's Adventures in History," *Boston Globe*, October 10, 2004.

41 "Everlasting peace is a dream": Michael A. Ledeen, *Machiavelli on Modern Leadership: Why Machiavelli's Iron Rules Are as Timely and Important Today as Five Centuries Ago* (New York: St. Martin's Press, 1999), p. 71.

42 Only days before the invasion of Iraq: Edsall and Milbank, op. cit.

42 the late Leo Strauss, the University of Chicago political philosopher: Shadia Drury, *Leo Strauss and the American Right* (New York: Palgrave Macmillan, 1997) p. 3.

43 "a theorist . . . much admired by Strauss": ibid.

44 "But Strauss remains mesmerized": Alan Gilbert, "Worse Than Any of Us Could Imagine," unpublished manuscript, 2006.

44 The most startling expression: Leo Strauss, *Gesammelte Schriften, Bd. 3: Hobbes' politische Wissenschaft und zugehörige Schriften, Briefe*, ed. Heinrich Meier (Berlin: Metzler Verlag, 2001), pp. 624–25.

45 The majority of the Jewish community: *Washington Post*, September 22, 2004.

46 The most fateful collaborations: Seymour Hersh, "Moving Targets," *New Yorker*, December 15, 2003.

47 Journalist William Arkin reported: *Los Angeles Times*, October 16, 2003.

47 By the spring of 2006, Cambone and Boykin: Seymour Hersh, "The Gray Zone," *New Yorker*, May 24, 2004.

48 Keeping such close quarters with religious zealots: David Frum, *The Right Man: An Inside Account of the Bush White House* (New York: Random House, 2003), pp. 3–4.

48 As long ago as 1986, Irving Kristol shocked: Irving Kristol, "Room for Darwin and the Bible," *New York Times*, September 30, 1986.

49 Fundamentalist support for Israel: Sarah Posner, "Pastor Strangelove," *American Prospect*, June 2006.

49 Although they are atheists and agnostics: Melanie Phillips, "The Politics of Progress," *Jewish Chronicle*, January 1, 2005.

49 described the late professor as an atheist and elitist: Robert Locke, "Leo Strauss, Conservative Mastermind," *Frontpage Magazine.com*, May 31, 2002.

50 Ledeen derives the same essential message: Michael A. Ledeen, "Machiavelli for Moderns," AEI Bradley Lecture, January 1, 2000, http://www.aei.org/publications/filter.all,pubID.18971/pubdetail.asp.

50 "Specifically, many conservative evangelicals fervently believe": Michelle Goldberg, *Kingdom Coming* (New York: Norton, 2006).

51 "George Bush was not elected": William M. Arkin, "The Pentagon Unleashes a Holy Warrior," *Los Angeles Times*, October 16, 2003.

51 "He knew George Bush had the ability to lead": Dana Milbank, "Religious Right Finds Its Center in Oval Office," *Washington Post*, December 24, 2001.

51 Former New York mayor Rudolph Giuliani: Joe Conason, "Is George W. Bush God's President?", *New York Observer*, January 14, 2002.

2. LAWLESSNESS AND ORDER

57 Under Bush's order: Philip A. Gagner, "The Bush Administration's Claim That Even Citizens Can Be Brought Before Military Tribunals," *FindLaw*, December 26, 2001.

58 "We are letting George Bush get away with": William Safire, "Seizing Dictatorial Power," *New York Times*, November 15, 2001.

58 For three weeks: Steven Mufson, "Leahy, Hatch Seek Ashcroft Testimony on Civil Liberties," *Washington Post*, November 26, 2001.

58 As Senator Robert Byrd of West Virginia . . . recalled: *Congressional Record*, September 17, 2002, pp. S8644–49.

59 When . . . Louis Freeh approached the attorney general: Joe Conason, "Ashcroft's Failures Deserve a Hearing," *New York Observer*, June 7, 2002.

60 That assignment fell to a group: Richard B. Schmitt, "Patriot Act Author Has Concerns," *Los Angeles Times*, November 30, 2003.

60 Reading through its provisions: Dahlia Lithwick and Julia Turner, "A Guide to the Patriot Act," *Slate*, September 8, 2003.

62 As Lincoln Caplan . . . observed: Lincoln Caplan, "Secret Affairs," *Legal Affairs*, November-December 2002.

62 Ashcroft called for instantaneous passage: Statement of U.S. Senator Russ Feingold, October 25, 2001.

63 The *Times* revealed that Ashcroft and Dinh: Fox Butterfield, "Justice Dept. Bars Use of Gun Checks in Inquiry," *New York Times*, December 6, 2001.

63 An al Qaeda handbook: Unsigned editorial, "Gun Loopholes and Terror," *Christian Science Monitor*, May 28, 2003.

64 During the weeks that followed the attacks: U.S. Department of Justice, Inspector General's Report on the September 11th Response, June 2003.

65 When the Justice Department's own inspector general: Nat Hentoff, "Is Ashcroft Fit for Office?", *Village Voice*, June 27, 2003.

66 And then he responded to his critics: Dan Eggan, "Ashcroft Defends Anti-Terrorism Steps," *Washington Post*, December 6, 2001.

67 Originally, Bush had wanted to name Marc Racicot: Mike Allen, "GOP Conservatives Derailed Racicot for Attorney General," *Washington Post*, January 2, 2001.

68 More significantly, he was a member of the Council for National Policy: Michelle Goldberg, "Fundamentally Unsound," *Salon.com*, July 29, 2002.

69 Someone had found a bottle of Crisco oil: John Ashcroft, *Lessons from a Father to His Son* (New York: Nelson Books, 1998), p. 179.

70 "Unique among the nations": ibid.

70 "A regent is one who governs": Frederick Clarkson, "No Longer Without Sheep," *Public Eye*, Spring 1994.

71 The directors of the Federalist Society include: www.fed-soc.org.

71 Lino Graglia, who describes himself as "far right": Adam Cohen, "Hell Hath No Fury Like a Conservative Who Is Victorious," *New York Times*, November 24, 2002.

72 In a sense, however, the Federalist Society's purpose: Jerry Landay, "The Conservative Cabal That's Transforming American Law," *Washington Monthly*, March 2000.

72 At the request of the White House, Yoo began: Peter Slevin, "Scholar Stands By Post-9/11 Writings on Torture, Domestic Eavesdropping," *Washington Post*, December 26, 2005.

73 As Bradford Berenson, then an associate White House counsel: Tim Golden, "After Terror, a Secret Rewriting of Military Law," *New York Times*, October 24, 2004.

74 Douglas Feith . . . under secretary of defense for policy: Ken Silverstein, "US Military Lawyers Felt 'Shut Out' of Prison Policy," *Los Angeles Times*, May 14, 2004.

74 Yoo's key memorandum on the Geneva Conventions: John Barry, Michael Hirsh, and Michael Isikoff, "The Roots of Torture," *Newsweek*, May 24, 2004.

74 The strongest endorsement of Yoo's approach: ibid.

76 A clever blogger known only as Julius Civitatus: http://img70.imageshack.us/my.php?image=aproval vs alert chart NEW.gif.

76 The next day, Ashcroft convened: Dan Eggen and Susan Schmidt, " 'Dirty Bomb' Plot Uncovered, U.S. Says; Suspected Al Queda Operative Held as 'Enemy Combatant'," *Washington Post*, June 11, 2002.

77 So was Yaser Esam Hamdi: Dahlia Lithwick, "Never Mind, Hamdi Wasn't Bad After All," *Slate*, September 23, 2004.

78 And for good measure: D. Mark Jackson, "Has Attorney General John Ashcroft, in Alleged Terrorism Cases, Violated Government Ethics Rules Governing Prosecutors' Comments About the Accused?" *Findlaw.com*, January 30, 2003.

79 "I'm pretty sure that's an argument": Joe Conason, "The Torture Tutor," *American Prospect*, February 5, 2006.

80 "Silberman's own career": ibid.

81 Silberman's open displays of partisan bias: Lawrence E. Walsh, *Firewall: The Iran-Contra Conspiracy and Coverup* (New York: Norton, 1997), p. 236.

81 David Brock has said that: David Brock, *Blinded by the Right: The Conscience of an Ex-Conservative* (New York: Crown, 2002), p. 146.

82 Alluding to the power to collect . . . information: Joe Conason, "The Torture Tutor," *American Prospect*, February 5, 2006.

82 "The pattern that emerges": Gene Healy and Timothy Lynch, *Power Surge: The Constitutional Record of George W. Bush* (Washington, D.C.: Cato Institute, 2006).

83 As the legal scholar David Cole observed: "What Bush Wants to Hear," *New York Review of Books*, November 17, 2005.

84 "What saved Gonzales from being completely contemptible": Bill Minutaglio, *The President's Counselor: The Rise to Power of Alberto Gonzales* (New York: HarperCollins, 2006).

84 When the Senate Judiciary Committee questioned him: Dan Eggen and R. Jeffrey Smith, "Gonzales Defends His White House Record; Nominee Questioned on Detainee Policies," *Washington Post*, January 7, 2005.

86 Yet somehow the governor's counsel: Alan Berlow, "The Texas Clemency Memos," *Atlantic Monthly*, July/August 2003.

86 And he misled the senators: Carol D. Leonnig, "Gonzales Is Challenged on Wiretaps; Feingold Says Attorney General Misled Senators in Hearings," *Washington Post*, January 31, 2006.

88 The quiet but powerful dissent within the military: Joe Conason, "Officers and Veterans Defy Bush's Neocons," *New York Observer*, August 8, 2005.

90 Bush responded with yet another reiteration: Charlie Savage, "Bush Challenges Hundreds of Laws," *Boston Globe*, April 30, 2006.

90 But the use of the signing statement: "Using Presidential Signing Statement to Make Fuller Use of the President's Constitutionally Assigned Role in the Process of Enacting Law," U.S. Department of Justice, Office of Legal Counsel, by Samuel A. Alito, February 5, 1986, http://www.archives.gov/news/samuel-alito/accession-060-89-269/Acc060-89-269-box6-SG-LSWG-AlitotoLSWG-Feb1986.pdf.

3. STATE SECRETS AND UNOFFICIAL PROPAGANDA

96 Two weeks after September 11, the president's press secretary: Press briefing by Ari Fleischer, September 26, 2001, http://www.whitehouse.gov/news/releases/2001/09/20010926-5.html.

97 The White House responded to the flap: Bill Carr and Felicity Barringer, "In Patriotic Time, Dissent Is Muted," *New York Times*, September 28, 2001.

97 For two weeks following the terror attack: Mike Allen, "White House Drops Claim of Threat to Bush," *Washington Post*, September 27, 2001.

98 Replete with scenes and dialogue created to burnish: Tom Shales, "Dull Paean; Showtime's 'DC 9/11' Is Shameless Bush-Booster," *Washington Post*, September 6, 2003.

99 J. Hoberman offered a more telling parallel: J. Hoberman, "Lights, Camera, Exploitation," *Village Voice*, September 2, 2003.

99 Before production began, Chetwynd submitted his script: Paul Farhi, " 'D.C. 9/11' Spins Tale of President on Tragic Day; Showtime Docudrama Depicts a Defiant, Decisive Bush," *Washington Post*, June 19, 2003.

100 "slow-walked and stone-walled": Timothy J. Burger, "9/11 Probe: Aiming High," *Time*, February 3, 2003.

101 Among the reforms that sprang forth from Congress: Thomas S. Blanton, "Battle Ongoing to Fight Secrecy in Government; Cheney, Rumsfeld, Scalia Opposed FOIA Improvements in '74," *Charlotte Observer*, December 2, 2004.

102 "I believe that truth is the glue": Gerald R. Ford's Remarks on Taking the Oath of Office as President, August 9, 1974, http://www.ford.utexas.edu/library/speeches/740001.htm.

102 Endorsing their effort to kill the reforms: "Supreme Court Justice Scalia Fought Against the Freedom of Information Act," see memos reproduced at http://www.thememoryhole.org/foi/scalia foia.htm.

103 "We just don't give out that kind of information": Robert Dreyfuss, "Vice Squad," *American Prospect*, May 2006.

103 "I really think they think": Mark Silva, "Bush Imposes Thick Veil of Secrecy," *Chicago Tribune*, April 30, 2006.

103 a White House subsidiary of the oil, coal, nuclear, and utility industries: Howard Fineman and Michael Isikoff, "Big Energy at the Table," *Newsweek*, May 14, 2001.

104 The chief lobbyist for the electric utilities: *Newsweek*, March 26, 2001.

105 The administration's defiance: Charles Lane, "High Court Hears Case on Cheney Energy Panel; White House Argues for Confidentiality," *Washington Post*, April 28, 2004.

106 But Olson appealed to the Supreme Court: Charles Lane, "High Court Backs Vice President; Energy Documents Shielded for Now," *Washington Post*, June 25, 2004.

106 In the GAO lawsuit: Charles Lane, "High Court Will Review Ruling on Cheney Task Force Records; Decision a Blow to Groups Seeking Information on Energy Policy," *Washington Post*, December 16, 2003.

107 Attorney General Ashcroft issued a sweeping new directive: Karen Branch-Brioso, "Attorney General Has Seized the Reins," *St. Louis Post-Dispatch*, May 19, 2002; and http://www.usdoj.gov/oip/foia post/2001foiapost19.htm.

107 The Ashcroft memo was followed: *Secrecy in the Bush Administration*, United States House of Representatives Committee on Government Reform, Minority Staff, September 14, 2004, p. 6.

108 "The Bush Justice Department does not seem": ibid., p. 29.

109 On November 1, 2001, just two weeks: ibid., p. 31.

109 Alberto Gonzales, who drafted the executive order: Elisabeth Bumiller, "Bush Keeps Grip on Presidential Papers," *New York Times*, November 2, 2001.

110 In fact, according to Bruce Craig: *Organization of American Historians Newsletter*, August 2002, http://www.oah.org/pubs/nl/2002aug/craig.html.

111 As *Slate* magazine's Fred Kaplan noted: Fred Kaplan, "Secret Again: The Absurd Scheme to Reclassify Documents," *Slate*, February 23, 2006.

111 The irony of all these efforts: Remarks of J. William Leonard, Director, Information Security Oversight Office (ISOO) at the National Classification Management Society's (NCMS) Annual Training Seminar, June 15, 2004, http://ww.archives.gov/isoo/speeches-and-articles/ncms-2004.html.

113 The officer who performed that important service: Truth from These Podia: Summary of a Study of Strategic Influence, Perception Management, Strategic Information Warfare, and Strategic Psychological Operations in Gulf War II, USAF Col. Sam Gardiner,

Ret., October 8, 2003, www.usnews.com/usnews/politics/whispers/documents/truth 1.pdf.

115 Indeed, Rumsfeld indicated: Secretary Rumsfeld Media Availability En Route to Chile, November 18, 2002, http://www.defenselink.mil/transcripts/2002/t11212002_t1118sd2.htm.

116 To skeptics, these offices seemed: Daniel Schulman, "Mind Games," *Columbia Journalism Review*, May/June 2006.

116 The largest and most powerful of these organizations: James Bamford, "The Man Who Sold the War," *Rolling Stone*, November 17, 2005.

117 Initially operating under the name Iraqex, Ltd.: Jeff Gerth, "Military's Information War Is Vast and Often Secretive," *New York Times*, December 11, 2005.

118 "The mysterious firm appeared to be run": Patrick Foster and Tim Reid, "Godalming Geek Made Millions Running the Pentagon's Propaganda War in Iraq," *Times Online* (London), December 24, 2005.

119 "The problem was": Daniel Schulman, "Mind Games," *Columbia Journalism Review*, May/June 2006.

119 Actually, the correct number: *Media Contracts: Activities and Financial Obligations for Seven Federal Departments*, Government Accountability Office, January 2006.

120 Government advertising and PR campaigns ranged: "GAO Finds Government Departments Spend More Than $1.6 Billion in Public Relations and Advertising Contracts," Rep. Henry A. Waxman, February 13, 2006.

120 Even more disturbing is the growing epidemic: Andrew Buncombe, "Bush Planted Fake News on American TV," *The Independent* (London), May 29, 2006.

121 The Bush administration's propensity: Joe Conason, "Don't Like the News? Buy Your Own," *New York Observer*, December 12, 2005.

123 Not long after Bush appointed Kenneth Tomlinson: Joe Conason, "Must-Flee TV: The GOP on PBS," *New York Observer*, May 9, 2005.

124 It was in Tomlinson's engineering: Joe Conason, "Public Broadcast (igation)," *American Prospect*, June 6, 2005.

125 Tomlinson moved on before he could be humiliated: *All Things Considered*, National Public Radio, September 8, 2006.

126 Bush replaced him: Paul Farhi, "Major GOP Donor Favored as Next CPB Chairman," *Washington Post*, July 15, 2005.

126 "We love your show": "As O'Reilly Let CPB's Tomlinson Deny White House Contacts, Tomlinson Gushed," Media Matters for America, May 13, 2005, www.mediamatters.org/items/200505130006.

127 As a news executive: David Brock, *The Republican Noise Machine: Right-Wing Media and How It Corrupts Democracy*, (New York: Crown, 2004), pp. 230–34.

127 "It was because of our coverage": The Hotline, *National Journal*, November 19, 2002.

127 Citing what they call "the Fox effect": Richard Morin, "The Fox News Effect," *Washington Post*, May 4, 2006.

127 Aside from profit, which only began to flow: Estimates derived by author from annual reports of Fox Entertainment Group, Inc.

128 The Fox message is not subtle: "Cavuto teaser," Media Matters for America, May 23, 2006, http://mediamatters.org/items/200605230003.

128 Fox anchors simply regurgitate: "Fox's Angle Adopted Administration Explanation," February 6, 2006, Media Matters for America, http://mediamatters.org/items/20060209000.

128 when anchor David Asman referred: "Fox Freudian Slip," May 25, 2005, Media Matters for America, http://mediamatters.org/items/200505250007.

128 "I was told": United Press International, April 28, 2006.

129 Answering a question about the president's position: Press briefing by Tony Snow, May 17, 2006, www.whitehouse.gov/news/releases/ 2006/05/20060517-4.html.

129 The special Fox connection is reminiscent: Lewis, pp. 283–84.

130 Fox News personalities and guests: *Your World with Neil Cavuto,* June 29, 2006, http://www.foxnews.com/story/0,2933,201549,00 .html; and *Hannity & Colmes,* June 23, 2006, http://www.foxnews .com/story/0,2933,201002,00.html (among others).

130 After the *Times* reported: "Fox & Friends co-host Kilmeade advocated 'Office of Censorship,'" June 29, 2006, http://mediamatters.org/items/200606290009.

130 Specifically, it can be found in: Gabriel Schoenfeld, "Has the *New York Times* Violated the Espionage Act?", *Commentary,* March 2006.

4. THE CORPORATE STATE OF GRACE

136 That was why Thomas Paine: Thomas Paine, *Agrarian Justice* (Philadelphia: Benjamin Franklin Bache, 1797), http://www .ssa.gov/history/tpaine3.html.

136 and why Benjamin Franklin, a rich businessman: William H. Gates and Chuck Collins, *Wealth and Our Commonwealth* (Boston: Beacon Press, 2004), p. 12.

137 His elected dictator Buzz Windrip: Lewis, pp. 31–33.

138 Although the Liberty League purported to be: David Pietrusza, "New Deal Nemesis," *Reason,* January 1978.

138 Late in 1934, the League was implicated: "Gen. Butler Bares 'Fascist Plot' to Seize Government by Force; Says Bond Salesman, as Representative of Wall St. Group, Asked Him to Lead Army of 500,000 in March on Capital—Those Named Make Angry Denials—Dickstein Gets Charge," *New York Times,* November 21, 1934

139 K Street Project: Gail Russell Chaddock, "Republicans Take Over K Street," *Christian Science Monitor*, August 29, 2003.

139 military-industrial complex: Eisenhower Farewell Address, January 17, 1961, http://mcadams.posc.mu.edu/ike.htm.

139 The biggest beneficiary of privatized security contracts: Bill Sizemore and Joanne Kimberlin, "Profitable Patriotism," *Virginian-Pilot* (Norfolk, Va.), July 24, 2006.

140 "Corporatist rule is exemplified": Eric Pianin, "Executive: 'Big Coal' Swayed Bush; Industry Lobbied Against Pledge to Reduce Emissions," *Washington Post*, May 23, 2002; Dana Milbank and Justin Blum, "Document Says Oil Chiefs Met with Cheney Task Force," *Washington Post*, November 16, 2005; Wayne Slater, "Energy Firms Buy Bush Favors, Critics Say," *Dallas Morning News*, August 30, 2004.

140 Kelliher wrote no white papers: Nicholas Confessore, "Welcome to the Machine: How the GOP Disciplined K Street and Make Bush Supreme," *Washington Monthly*, July 1, 2003.

141 Before the end of George W. Bush's first term: Anne C. Mulkern, "When Advocates Become Regulators," *Denver Post*, May 24, 2004.

141 "In the Bush administration": ibid.

142 Tom DeLay cultivated: Environmental Working Group report, May 1995, http://www.ewg.org/reports/Proj_Relief/Relief.html; and Michael Weisskopf and David Maraniss, "Forging an Alliance for Deregulation," *Washington Post*, March 12, 1995.

142 Then, in 1989, Robertson decided to resurrect: Joe Conason, "The Religious Right's Quiet Revival," *Nation*, April 27, 1992.

143 "We want to see a working majority": ibid.

143 "unknowingly and unwittingly . . .": Pat Robertson, *The New World Order* (Dallas: Word Publishing, 1991), p. 37.

144 The following summer, in July 1992: Joe Conason, "A Political Story—Chapter and Verse," *Columbia Journalism Review*, July/August 1993.

144 the Christian Coalition had plunged: Bill Sizemore, "Once Powerful Christian Coalition Teeters on Insolvency," *Virginian-Pilot* (Chesapeake, Va.), October 8, 2005.

145 Karl Rove, whose friends knew: Glenn Thrush, "Rove Denies 'Demon' Rumors," *Newsday*, September 8, 2006.

146 Sometime in 1997: James Moore and Wayne Slater, *The Architect: Karl Rove and the Master Plan for Absolute Power* (New York: Crown, 2006), p. 83.

147 In October 1999, the Texas governor: ABC News, May 2, 2006, http://abcnews.go.com/Politics/print?id=121170.

148 Named along with LaHaye: Sarah Posner, "Secret Society," *The Gadflyer*, February 21, 2005.

149 While the CNP enjoys tax-exempt status: ibid.

149 Skipp Porteous, a civil liberties activist: Skipp Porteous, "Bush's Secret Religious Pandering," *Freedom Writer*, September/October 2000, http://www.publiceye.org/ifas/fw/0009/bush.html.

150 Early in his presidency: Rob Gowland, "Dominion Over Heaven and Earth," *Guardian* (UK), April 13, 2005.

150 Perhaps the most disconcerting evidence: Rick Pearlstein, "The Divine Calm of George W. Bush," *Village Voice*, May 3, 2004.

151 The Federalist Society's chairman: www.fed-soc.org.

151 After Justice Sandra Day O'Connor announced: Jeffrey H. Birnbaum and Thomas B. Edsall, "Business Pushes Its Own Brand of Justice," *Washington Post*, July 9, 2005.

152 When Knight-Ridder Newspapers examined: Stephen Henderson and Howard Mintz, "Review of Cases Shows Alito to Be Staunch Conservative," *Philadelphia Inquirer*, December 4, 2005.

152 So well synchronized were the business lobbyists and religious rightists: "Alito Supporters, Foes, Start Ad Campaigns," *USA Today*, November 17, 2005.

152 The wording of the ads: ibid.

153 "It's the season when": Fred Barbash, "The Committee for Justice, New Radio Ad," *washingtonpost.com*, December 6, 2005.

153 Although Rove and Reed left no visible fingerprints: Joshua Green, "Karl Rove in a Corner," *Atlantic Monthly*, November 2004.

154 McCain had his revenge: Joe Conason, "McCain in 2008?", *Salon .com*, March 3, 2006.

154 But the *Washington Post*'s first investigative article: Susan Schmidt, "A Jackpot from Indian Gaming Tribes," *Washington Post*, February 22, 2004.

155 Known to his peers as "Casino Jack": Philip Shenon, "Inquiries of Top Lobbyist Shine Unwelcome Light in Congress," *New York Times*, April 11, 2005.

155 For a skillful hypocrite like Reed: ibid.

156 The conditions endured by the women workers: Thomas Korosec, "Our Man in Saipan," *Dallas Observer*, February 19, 1998.

157 Yet such unsavory parallels don't disturb: Alexander Bolton, "DeLay Backers Draw Up Plan to Hit Back," *The Hill*, March 30, 2005.

157 At one of many fundamentalist meetings: Joe Conason, "Let Us Prey," *Salon.com*, January 6, 2006.

158 The former majority leader stood before the House: Federal News Service, April 4, 2006.

158 "Nothing illegal about that at all": Mike Allen, "Tom DeLay Tells Why He's Quitting," *Time*, April 3, 2006.

160 Senate majority leader Bill Frist, a former heart and lung surgeon: Charles Babington, "Viewing Videotape, Frist Disputes Fla. Doctors' Diagnosis of Schiavo," *Washington Post*, March 19, 2005.

161 "I'm convinced the best thing government can do": Sarah Posner, "With God on His Side," *American Prospect*, November 2005.

162 "The alliance of Mammon and the religious right: Marshall Wittman, "Moose on the Loose," *Blueprint*, October 7, 2004.

163 Randy Brinson, an Alabama physician: Amy Sullivan, "When Would Jesus Bolt?" *Washington Monthly*, April 1, 2006.

5. THE REVENGE OF NIXON'S HEIRS

168 Broadly speaking, he dismissed congressional authority: Arthur Schlesinger Jr., *The Imperial Presidency* (New York: Mariner Books, 2004), p. 255.

168 He circumvented Congress in his conduct of war: ibid., p. 378.

168 Nixon in hindsight sounded almost naïve: Interview with David Frost, May 19, 1977, http://www.landmarkcases.org/nixon/nixon view.html.

168 The register of indictments against the Nixon gang: See J. Anthony Lukas, *Nightmare: The Underside of the Nixon Years* (New York: Viking Press, 1976), pp. 522–32.

169 "healthy right-wing exuberants": Transcript of taped White House conversation between Nixon and Charles Colson (who later went to prison), January 8, 1973, http://www.hpol.org/transcript.php?id=100.

169 "fascist thugs like G. Gordon Liddy": G. Gordon Liddy, *Will* (New York: St. Martin's Press, reprint edition, 1996), p. 59. Note that Liddy refers to himself and his FBI colleagues as "an elite corps, America's protective echelon, its *Schutzstaffel*," or Nazi SS.

170 "If the president, for example, approves something": Interview with David Frost, May 19, 1977, http://www.landmarkcases.org/nixon/nixonview.html.

171 It was Nixon who rescued George Herbert Walker Bush: Kitty Kelley, *The Family: The Real Story of the Bush Dynasty* (New York: Doubleday, 2004), pp. 244–46.

171 "In thirty-four years, I have repeatedly seen": ABC News *This Week*, January 27, 2002.

172 "I do have the view that over the years: Vice President's Remarks to the Traveling Press, Air Force Two, En Route to Oman, December 20, 2005, http://www.whitehouse.gov/news/releases/2005/12/20051220-9.html.

172 "They're focused on restoring": Jane Mayer, "The Hidden Power," *New Yorker*, July 3, 2006.

172 The vice president shares his autocratic convictions: James Mann, *Rise of the Vulcans* (New York: Viking, 2004), pp. 56–72.

173 According to Bradley: T. D. Allman, "The Curse of Dick Cheney," *Rolling Stone*, August 25, 2004.

173 "As a leader of the College Republicans": John W. Dean, *Worse than Watergate: The Secret Presidency of George W. Bush* (New York: Little, Brown, 2004), pp. 4–5.

173 In August 1973, exactly a year before Nixon's resignation: "RNC Probes Official as Teacher of Tricks," *Washington Post*, August 10, 1973.

174 "George H. W. Bush, then the chairman": James Moore and Wayne Slater, *Bush's Brain: How Karl Rove Made George W. Bush Presidential* (New York: John Wiley, 2003), pp. 133–35.

174 "The tough, devious young operative": David Greenberg, *Nixon's Shadow: The History of an Image* (New York: Norton, 2003), p. 204.

175 "I never really liked Nixon *until* Watergate": Rick Perlstein, "The Conservative Movement Now," *HuffingtonPost.com*, December 5, 2005, www.huffingtonpost.com/rick-perlstein/i-didnt-like-nixon-_b_11735.html.

175 Congress shall, immediately upon our inauguration: Lewis, p. 63.

176 "the unitary presidency": Stephen Holmes, "John Yoo's Tortured Logic," *Nation*, May 1, 2006.

177 "The government may be justified": James Risen and Eric Licht-blau, "Bush Lets U.S. Spy on Callers Without Courts," *New York Times*, December 16, 2005.

177 Congress could not place any "limits: Memorandum Opinion for the Deputy Counsel to the President, by John C. Yoo, Deputy Assistant Attorney General, Justice Department Office of Legal Counsel, September 25, 2001, http://www.usdoj.gov/olc/warpowers925.htm.

178 "The powers of the presidency have been eroded": Jim Hoagland, "Two Leaders' Power Failures: Bush and Putin, Against the Tide," *Washington Post*, March 9, 2006.

179–180 Huston's new task force came up with a more ambitious program: Lukas, *Nightmare*, pp. 33–36.

180 The FISA statute, signed by President Jimmy Carter: *The Foreign Intelligence Surveillance Act: An Overview of the Statutory Framework and Recent Judicial Decisions*, by Elizabeth B. Bazan, Congressional Research Service, April 21, 2005.

181 "Now, by the way . . . any time you hear the . . . government talking about wiretap": Remarks by the President in a Conversation on the USA Patriot Act, White House press release, April 20, 2004, http://www.whitehouse.gov/news/releases/2004/04/20040420-2.html.

182 NSA had tapped directly into the main arteries: Eric Lichtblau, "Officials Want to Expand Review of Domestic Spying," *New York Times*, December 24, 2005.

182 The president himself reacted angrily: Press conference of the President, White House news release, December 19, 2005, http://www.whitehouse.gov/news/releases/2005/12/20051219-2.html.

183 Five months later, in May 2006: Shane Harris and Murray Waas, "Justice Department Probe Foiled," *National Journal*, May 25, 2006.

183 "You can have the President": Jack M. Balkin, "Tales from the Unitary Executive Part II," *Balkinization*, July 18, 2006, http://balkin.blogspot.com/2006/07/tales-from-unitary-executive-part-ii.html.

184 Specifically, Gonzales pointed to the Authorization to Use Military Force: Prepared Statement of Attorney General Alberto R. Gonzales, Senate Judiciary Committee, February 6, 2006, http://www .usdoj.gov/ag/speeches/2006/ag speech 060206.html.

184 "Gonzales admitted that in the fall of 2001": Press briefing by Attorney General Alberto Gonzales and General Michael Hayden, White House press release, December 19, 2005, http://www.white house.gov/news/releases/2005/12/20051219-1.html.

185 "I'm not going to rule it out": Eric Lichtblau, "Gonzales Suggests Legal Basis for Domestic Eavesdropping," *New York Times*, April 7, 2006.

185 "Let me be as clear as I can": Adam Nagourney, "Rove Lays Out Road Map for Republicans in Fall Elections," *New York Times*, January 20, 2006.

186 Ann Coulter repeatedly called: "Coulter: 'I prefer a firing squad' for NY *Times*' Keller," Media Matters for America, July 13, 2006, http://mediamatters.org/items/200607130003.

186 San Francisco radio host Melanie Morgan: Joe Garofoli, "New Chapter in Battle of Words Over Tracking Terrorist Financing; House Plans Debate to Praise Program, Snipe at Exposers," *San Francisco Chronicle*, June 29, 2006.

186 "Let me tell you something, folks": "Limbaugh: 'If we get hit again' by terrorists, blame 'Leahy, Biden, Durbin, Boxer, Kennedy, Reid," *Newsweek, Time, The New York Times*, and Amnesty International'," *The Rush Limbaugh Show*, June 14, 2005, http://mediamatters .org/items/200506150006.

186 Bill O'Reilly has repeatedly accused: "O'Reilly on ACLU: 'I think they're a terrorist group. . . . I think they're terrorists'," Media Matters for America, March 3, 2005, http://mediamatters.org/items/ 200503030007.

187 Frank Gaffney, the neoconservative defense analyst: Max Blumenthal, "Princeton Tilts Right," *Nation*, March 13, 2006.

188 Not only did this program manifestly flout: Bob Secter and Jon Van, "Lawyer," *Chicago Tribune,* May 13, 2006.

188 In response to that second embarrassing story: Stephen J. Hedges and Mark Silva, "Bush: No Laws Were Broken; Millions of Phone Records Reportedly Sold to NSA," *Chicago Tribune,* May 12, 2006.

188 A former NSA employee named Russell Tice: ibid.

188 If such an ambitious concept seems familiar: David Cole, "Uncle Sam Is Watching You," *New York Review of Books,* November 18, 2004.

189 When he ran the National Security Council: *Final Report of the Independent Counsel for Iran/Contra Matters,* Part IV, Chapter 3, August 4, 1993, http://www.fas.org/irp/offdocs/walsh/chap 03.htm.

189 Press secretary Ari Fleischer unwittingly demonstrated: Press briefing, White House press release, February 25, 2002, http://www.white house.gov/news/releases/2002/02/20020225-16.html#2.

190 Or as Poindexter put it: *Overview of the Information Awareness Office,* Remarks by Dr. John Poindexter at DARPATech 2002 Conference, August 2, 2002, http://www.fas.org/irp/agency/dod/poindexter .html.

190 This overweening scheme raised alarms: William Safire, "You Are a Suspect," *New York Times,* November 14, 2002.

190 In October 2003, more than a year after the program: Cole, "Uncle Sam Is Watching You."

191 "We will be describing this new effort": Shane Harrison, "TIA Lives On," *National Journal,* February 23, 2006.

191 Intelligence sources have informed: Michael Hirsh, *Newsweek* Web Exclusive, *MSNBC.com,* February 8, 2006.

191 Run mostly by private consulting companies: William Arkin, "Telephone Records Are Just the Tip of NSA's Iceberg," *washingtonpost .com,* May 12, 2006.

192 The Pentagon had established a secret domestic counterintelligence program: Lisa Myers, Douglas Pasternak, Rich Gardella, and the NBC Investigative Unit, "Is the Pentagon Spying on Americans? Secret Database Obtained by NBC News Tracks 'Suspicious' Domestic Groups," *MSNBC.com*, December 14, 2005.

192 TALON investigators filed reports: Michael Isikoff, "The Other Big Brother: The Pentagon Has Its Own Domestic Spying Program. Even Its Leaders Say the Outfit May Have Gone Too Far," *Newsweek*, January 30, 2006.

193 An elderly protester named Gail Sredanovic: Matthew Rothschild, "Rumsfeld Spies on Quakers and Grannies," *Progressive*, December 16, 2005.

193 The TALON operations belonged to a secretive wing: Lisa Myers and the NBC Investigative Unit, "Pentagon Admits Errors in Spying on Protesters. NBC: Official says peaceful demonstrators names erased from database," *Newsweek* Web exclusive, March 10, 2006.

194 Citing the terrorist threat: Bill Berkowitz, "POLITICS-US: Green for Danger?", Interpress Service, February 2, 2006.

194 "I'm still somewhat shocked": Eric Lichtblau, "Large Volume of F.B.I. Files Alarms U.S. Activist Groups," *New York Times*, July 18, 2005.

195 When Operation TIPS . . . was reported: Jane Black, "Some TIPS for John Ashcroft: Mr. Attorney General, Forget Your Plan for a System to Promote Americans Spying on Americans. It Won't Work—And Is Un-American," *Business Week*, July 25, 2002.

195 But the Department of Homeland Security quietly: Ben Feller, "School Bus Drivers Join Terror Watch," Associated Press, February 19, 2006.

196 Those cases included a lawsuit by the Electronic Frontier Foundation: Ryan Singel, "AT&T Sued Over NSA Eavesdropping," *Wired*, January 31, 2006, http://www.wired.com/news/technology/0,70126-0.html.

196 The Senate Intelligence Committee . . . has spent more than two years: "The Intelligence Business," editorial, *New York Times*, May 7, 2006.

197 When Senator Arlen Specter: Letter from Senator Specter to the Vice President, June 7, 2006, http://civilliberty.about.com/od/waron terror/a/spectercheney.htm.

197 The noisy but abject Specter made a show: Walter Pincus, "Specter Offers Compromise on NSA Surveillance," *Washington Post*, June 9, 2006.

197 The bill created a new . . . system: "The Military Commissions Act of 2006," http://frwebgate.access.gpo.gov/cgi-bin/getdoc.cgi? dbname=109 cong bills&docid=f:s3930enr.txt.pdf.

198 Noting that the Democratic leadership: "Rushing Off a Cliff," editorial, *New York Times*, September 28, 2006.

198 No wonder the president feels free: Savage, *Boston Globe*, April 30, 2006.

199 The most important constitutional vindication: Linda Greenhouse, "The Ruling on Tribunals: The Overview; Justices, 5-3, Broadly Reject Bush Plan to Try Detainees," *New York Times*, June 30, 2006.

200 The *Hamdan* decision also rejected the argument: Ben Winograd, "Pondering Presidential Power," *Wall Street Journal*, June 29, 2006.

200 While Alito sought to soften his position: *Wall Street Journal*, January 5, 2006.

201 In 2004, he was willing to surrender: Fred Barbash, "Supreme Court Backs Civil Liberties in Terror Cases," *Washington Post*, June 29, 2004.

INDEX

3/07